Four Seasons

Four Seasons

THE FISHING DIARIES OF
Christopher Yates
JUNE 1977 - MARCH 1981

ELLESMERE
THE MEDLAR PRESS
2008

Published by the Medlar Press Limited,
The Grange, Ellesmere, Shropshire.
www.medlarpress.com

ISBN 978-1-899600-85-4

First published as a limited edition by the Medlar Press 1996
Second edition 2008
Text and Illustrations © Christopher Yates 1996
Design © The Medlar Press, 2008

Designed and typeset in 11/12.5 point Baskerville by Jonathan Ward-Allen.
Produced in England by
The Medlar Press Limited, Ellesmere, England.

CONTENTS

INTRODUCTION

Everyone, or at least almost every angler, knows that carp fishers are mad, but this diary, that was never intended for publication, reveals levels of madness that most carp fishers never reach. Not that there are many really sensational moments of craziness, it's simply that twenty years ago my obsession with carp and my absolute freedom to make the most of wonderful opportunities made it possible to indulge myself in carp fishing without com-promise. For instance, I was completely infatuated with a small, pretty, but unimpressive-looking pool called Redmire, and - because of my fortunate circumstances - was able to spend more time there than anyone else in its short history.

Of course I can dissociate myself from the angler who scribbled the diary because it concerns a period that is well and truly passed. I am not the same person anymore: I don't fish in the same way; I am not suffering from the same obsessions; I could not afford the time, or the money to dissolve so completely into a chosen water; life has led me in other equally compelling directions.

It is not my fault that the diary is now an open book. Jon Ward-Allen was in the middle of producing the Medlar edition of *Casting at the Sun* and, knowing that I always kept an angling diary, he asked if he could see it. He was simply curious to read what was going on between the more memorable events that I'd already written about in *Casting*, and having read it, he then, for reasons only known to himself, decided he must publish it, though he knew

I had strong reservations. I still have these reservations, not only because it is occasionally embarrassing, not only because much of the writing is hurried and sketchy, not only because the level of enthusiasm for any fish remains monotonously high, not only because several of the incidents recorded will already be familiar to many, but also because, even though I was only writing for myself, I never recorded my various historic encounters with gudgeon.

However, Jon is a very persuasive man - and he knows how much I like port . . .

Chris Yates, April 1996

Season 18

June 1977 - March 1978

OPENING NIGHT

Sheepwash (with the Golden Scale Club)

Two pitches had already been taken by the time I got to the bankside, and one of them was the one I might have chosen. But the recently cleared Sticks Pitch was vacant and it looked really promising. I set up my tackle, tossed in a few handfuls of 'Racing Beans', and after the usual ceremonies with Rick, Guy, Nick and Graham, we cast our baits - a few minutes late this year.

There was a coldish breeze from the north-east and no movement on the surface by carp. Prospects were not good so I had no qualms about sleeping till dawn.

At 4.45 a.m. I re-baited both rods and dropped one to the left, by an overhanging branch, and one to the right. At 5 a.m. the left-hand bait was taken. I was almost asleep again but the hiss of the silver paper had me over the rod. I struck - and missed! I cursed as I re-baited. Guy came along and I told him what had happened. Carp runs at Sheepwash are few and far between and I was not pleased. But as we were talking, the other silver paper flicked up. I struck immediately and this time connected. The fish dived along the bank to the right and tried to get round some overhanging trees. I bent hard and the rod top stabbed as if I were stuck into a big tench. For a while we thought it really *was* a tench. Then it came up to the top and we saw it was a long, lean, bright bronze and blue mirror-carp. It wasn't big but, like all Sheepwash carp, it fought like a tiger; round and round on the bottom till my arms were aching. Eventually it gave up and Guy netted it. On the bank we gasped at the size of the fins and tail. They were huge compared to the bulk of the fish. It reminded me of a big male tench, not only in its fight but also in its appearance. It weighed 7 lb. That was the only carp caught all day.

We went home for a steak and a bottle of wine in the evening and didn't get back till 11.0. But again, we weren't disturbed much through the dark hours. It was a much better night, though. Warm and very humid. It seemed, after the surprise sunshine of the 16th, that summer had returned, after nearly two weeks of cold weather. At about 3 a.m., I was roused by the silver paper on the right-hand rod. I struck and a fish dived down the bank. For a second or two I held him, then the line went slack. I'd lost him.

Overhead, a strange-sounding bird flew off into the dark. Perhaps he was laughing.

At 4.0 I had another run, but missed it. At 5.0 (again) I had a good run on the left-hand rod and this time connected. Again there was a fine struggle in the enclosed area of the Sticks Pitch. But this one was only 5 lb - however, it was a beautiful fish and, *deja vu*, it was a fully scaled mirror, like yesterday's. And again, it was the only carp taken on the lake that day.

Sunday, 19th June - Redmire Pool

Arrived at 2 p.m. with Roy, who was trembling in anticipation during the last twenty miles of the drive. The wind was cool and, as I'd predicted, was blowing in towards the dam. There was hardly any weed, in fact there was less than the 'bald' year of '72. We had a look up at the shallows and found a couple of goodish carp moving about. Not wanting to miss an early opportunity, we set up a rod each straight away. Roy fished with 'the Laboratory Special'[1] that I will have nothing to do with, and I fished with (paprika) Racing Beans[2]. For over an hour I watched a small number of carp passing close to the baits. Then, though it seemed to be warming up and the wind had died down, the carp disappeared.

As we had a cup of tea back under the trees, Ron Lally arrived. He set up in the Fence as I said I'd probably plump for Greenbanks, a favourite early season pitch - if the wind is right, which it wasn't. *[You should have fished in the 'Secret Swim'.]*

Ron had only had one carp before at Redmire, yet first cast with the Laboratory Special he hooked and landed a 21 lb 14 oz mirror! I couldn't believe it. Surely no bait could be that good. He hadn't even finished setting up his gear.

Back in the shallows I wondered what chance my Racing Beans had against such scientific devilry. I'd cast the Hardy Victor (8 foot 6 inch sea-trout rod, circa 1934) out on float only, a few yards from the platform on the fourth island. Suddenly, as I was sneaking off the island to have a look up the bank, there was a screech of the centre-pin reel. Leaping back on to the platform I picked up the rod and got my hand to the whizzing reel as a big bow wave arrowed out towards the weed-bed on the far side of the shallows. I slowed him and he veered first to the left and then made a long, screaming run down to the right, parallel to the far bank. I bent the little rod over and the carp rolled and swung round towards me. He came in, then ran out again making the reel sing. Eventually I had him splashing about next to the platform. I'd thought he might be a fair fish, though looking down

---

1. *In the close season the rest of the Redmire syndicate had devised a fiendish plan to bait up the pool with just one type of bait. This was an amino-acid-laced concoction that was marked under the brand name 'Black Magic'. I refused to even touch it.*

2. *'Racing Beans' were simply mixed bird food that I was originally introduced to by a man who bred racing pigeons. I would boil them for half an hour, with one dessert-spoon of paprika per pound.*

at him in the water he didn't look so impressive. Ron came up and netted him, and the carp expanded as we lifted him out. A prime common, in perfect condition. 15 lb. Best fish so far on the Hardy.

Monday, 20th June

Woke to a strong breeze in the willows above me. It was blowing away from me, down towards the dam. My pitch didn't look so promising.

After breakfast, a wash and the donning of an extra (the Redmire Special) pullover, I took the Hardy and a tin of sweetcorn round to the dam. I crept along it until I reached the overhanging bush about three quarters of the way across. It seemed the best place so I dropped the quill in under the rod top and scattered about half a dozen grains of corn around it.

I lent my elbows on the dam rail, watching the yellow quill as it bobbed in the incoming ripples. After about seven minutes it just sank steadily into the dark depths. I struck and felt a solid resistance. The fish circled deep down for a while, like all the other big ones I've hooked off the dam (during '72-'73). A huge cloud of bubbles rose up and then he began to go. The check on the centre-pin 'click-clicked', then screamed, and the carp headed steadily out and away to the Evening Pitch. I skipped across to the right-hand side of the dam, keeping a solid pressure on. The Hardy was standing the strain well, though I couldn't stop the carp till nearly twenty or thirty yards of line had streamed off the reel. I pumped him back for a way, then he turned and ran deep. I could feel the line biting through the sparse weed on the bottom. He turned more to the right but I stopped him so he ran out into deep water again. There was nowhere really dangerous he could get to from that corner of the dam. The water was deep and snag-free. The only hazard was the weed-filter platform, jutting out from the shallows near the overflow. If he got round that, goodbye carp. Suddenly, he charged towards it, but Ron was on hand with a big stone and the fish turned back. For nearly ten more minutes he kept low and deep, the rod hard over all the time. Then he began to circle close in and I knew the end was near. I saw him for the first time as I gave him a bit of sidestrain and brought him wallowing to the surface. He dived with a big swirl but I soon heaved him up again. Then I got him circling just below the surface and the net was held ready. He tried to get under the trailing branches in a last despairing effort, but I held him clear and Roy got him first swipe.

That was the most dramatic tussle I'd had with a carp for three years - much better than the fight with the 38 pounder, and that was on the same strength tackle. This fish was a common of 19 lb 11 oz and the lively debate amply made up for that lack of 5 ounces.

The wind stayed cool. By the evening, though, the sky had almost cleared and the air was still. It was cold though. Fishing from the dam again my breath showed like October.

Tuesday, 21st June

A perfect dawn. Still and misty with the light gradually strengthening as the horizon tilted eastward towards the sun. I took some photographs and then was just going to have a look off the dam when Roy called out. I ran round to the Willow Pitch and saw he was into a big fish. Through the mist a fin was showing like a black sail. But this carp was no fighter. It wallowed towards the net and came in like a baby as I leant out from the end of the punt. I said it must have been sedated by the bait, but Roy wasn't complaining. It was a wonderful-looking fish; Roy's first 20 - a 21 $^3/_4$ common, though it's a pity it came on the Laboratory Special. If the bait is truly irresistible then it'll make carp fishing worse than clinical: it will become predictable. It has been scientifically proven that carp are powerfully attracted by the secret chemical ingredients. So all you do is stick a lump of it on the hook, cast out, lie back and wait. I can't call that carp fishing. What happened to individual skills? Where's the satisfaction in hooking carp on a bait that's been proven to be infallible? Where's the mystery? Where's the fascination? Where's the interest? But at least I'm not going to use it. I'll stick to my own pattern of 'fly' and let the others buy magic ones ready made! *[You needn't have worried so much, you 'purist!'. In a week the carp had gone right of the muck. 29.6.77]*

I got back to my pitch after photographing the fish for Roy and found I'd had a run of about thirty feet on Racing Beans! Curses!

The sun began to get warm. It felt more like midsummer, at last, instead of autumn. After a midday siesta I went up to the shallows to find some big fish moving around. I could get the baits to them but they weren't showing any inclination to feed. Later on I found a great place to fish from a branch of a willow that grows right out in the weed-bed in the shallows. I was able to put my baits right on the noses of several 20 pounders, but they weren't interested. I remembered the opening week of '73: how Rod Hutchinson and I sneaked up to the shallows with broad beans and knew the fish were going to take them. I had a 17 and a 20 as well as numerous smaller fish, all from the very top swim. But now even a baby carp turned his nose up at my offerings. It wasn't the bait though, I'm sure. They just weren't up there to feed, just to bask in the sudden warmth and enjoy the quickly warming shallow water. Roy had a rod out on the other side and big fish were going straight over the Laboratory Special without a second glance. At least they won't take it when they're not hungry!

I went down to Symonds Yat to post a letter to Clare and buy a loaf of good bread. After tea, I tried to decide what to do. Big carp seemed to be shoaling off the islands, almost as if preparing to spawn (gudgeon were spawning in the little weed-bed in front of me). There were still movements of fish in the shallows. Should I move up to the '35'? Or fish deeper water, now that it seemed the north-eastern breeze was not going to change? A large carp surfaced not far from the baits as if in answer. Anyway, there was a perfect crescent moon hanging in the western sky. I'd stay where I was and watch it setting.

The sun had set red, over to my right at about 9.15. About an hour later the moon was in the trees on the opposite bank. For a while it looked just like the Magritte painting of a moon in a tree. Then it went down, orange, behind the high meadow. An owl called with that strange, monotonous call I heard on the Downs six years ago. Where the moon had set, another owl replied with the same soft 'ooo ooo'. Deep in my sleeping-bag, against the chill of the evening, I was soon asleep.

Wednesday, 22nd June

Nothing came to my baits in the night or the dawn. I woke late and had a look up in the shallows. There were carp everywhere. In the weed-bed, under the willows, but mostly under the far bank (naturally!).

I went round with the Hardy, and from the platform I had my polaroids misting up as several big carp went down over the bait right below the rod tip. But they were too canny to pick anything but the loose offerings. Further up it was the same. One huge mirror - possibly the 'Old 38' - put her nose down once or twice to pick up the odd grain, but she never went near the bait.

For two hours I waited, as big carp moved all round me. Only very occasionally would a really good fish go down for a few offerings. Delicately, the tail would tilt up, the pectorals held out straight, then the lips would go down so that the whole mouth covered the area around the desired morsel. The bigger the fish, the bigger the patch of mud covered by the mouth. The morsel would be sucked in very gently, leaving only a tiny puff of disturbed silt as the fish moved off. And always they moved off, never taking more than three beans.

At lunch-time I had a break for half an hour, then I crept back again. What an excellent stalking rod the Hardy is! It was no trouble as I crept through the tangle of willows and hawthorns on my way through the marshy undergrowth to Wasp Island. In the confined though very comfortable space, the rod was just the right length for flicking a bait out over the feeding, unsuspecting carp. Straight away I had a take, on a cockle Ron had given me. The line tightened. Then I saw the fish responsible. It must have weighed 2 lb, so I just kept a gentle pull on it until it had let go. Twice more this happened. Then a group of three big commons came in from the left. The biggest, a fish of around 25-30 lb by the look of him, saw the cockle on the bottom and went straight for it. As he took it in I struck. But the line was somehow caught round an underwater root right next to the carp. As I struck, so the carp was wrenched downwards. He didn't bolt, as I thought he would. He just looked a bit puzzled. Amazingly, the cockle, still on the hook, had been pulled out without the slightest sign that the fish knew anything about it. He just swam off unconcernedly. I almost had to pull for a break, as the hook was stuck on the root. Finally, it came free and I quickly cast again. I didn't have long to wait until a big mirror came straight out of the weed-bed, forty feet away, and made a bee-line for the cockle. Once more it took it without hesitation. I saw it go in, yet when I struck again the baited hook came flying out and the fish swam slowly off. Perhaps the bait was being taken even more timorously than usual, but I couldn't see anything unusual. I had a perfect view of proceedings as everything happened in crystal clear water only eighteen inches deep and only ten feet from the rod tip. I can't understand how it happened! Next time I was determined to wait a little longer. But there was no next time. On the other bank Ron had fallen asleep by his rod.

After a welcome few pints in the local at Langrove, I moved pitch to the Stile, putting out one rod on corn, one on Racing Beans and one on cockle. Three rods!! It was bad that I was so indecisive, but at least a choice of baits gives variety to a carp's diet.

The silver papers never moved!

Thursday, 23rd June

I woke just as the last planet began to fade in the rising light. A thick mist was on the water and the air was cold.

I made a pot of tea, then took a net and the Hardy up to the shallows. There was a fish feeding right in by the platform. Like a heron, I moved towards the disturbed water and dropped a cockle right into the cloud of bubbles. Nothing happened, and after a while the fish moved off. I cast twice more with the cockle, and while I waited so the sun came up over the hill and cast its beams through the mist.

I tossed out a handful of beans and in a while a fish began feeding over them. I kept low, re-baited with two grains and cast less than ten feet out. Then I sat back against the alder tree, watching the beams in the mist that were now taking on the form of a pyramid as the light spread towards me from a single chink in the willows on the far bank. Was there a stir on the surface? Under the willows, a big fish leapt right out of the water. The ripples came across to me. Again I thought I could see a stirring of water near the bait. Then the line angled out from the rod tip. I struck firmly, but not too hard, and a big bow wave went straight across the shallows. The sound of that centre-pin! The long, sustained screech had Ron out of his bothy in the Fence - and it takes a lot to wake Ron up at 5.30 in the morning. The vintage rod felt really tight and for the first few minutes it was completely hooped. The carp was right over by the far bank and I was worried in case he dived into one of the willow branches. Ron came opposite and prepared to do some frightening. But after that first tremendous rush I gained some control and began to ease my fish back. It felt very heavy, but I wasn't too sure about it as that run had been so fast. There was a lot of weed between me and the fish and that, I'm sure, put most of the solidity into the feel of things. Half way over, the carp surfaced, then charged away again. I put my fingers against the flying reel and slowly brought him to a water-churning stop. I thought he was going to give me more trouble than he did when I got him back to me, but he just circled around a bit, taking the odd few yards of line though never looking like diving into the sunken branches that lay to the right and left of me. I had the net already in the water and now I eased him gently over the mesh and smoothly lifted. He thrashed and splashed but I had him. Again his spirit was greater than his size, though he was a good fish. A brilliantly coloured common of 15 lb (again!). I left him in the water in the net while I went to get the Bronica. On the way I watched Roy hook and land his second 20. A common of 22 lb - again on the Laboratory Special. This was a much livelier specimen than his first and he had to sit down afterwards in the back of the punt and have a cigarette to calm his happily jangled nerves.

The day was very clear and bright. In the shadows the air was cool, but the sun was hot. All through the afternoon fish swam around lazily just below the surface. From the Island Tree I counted eighteen 20 pounders, some of them perhaps touching even 30 pounds. But there was nothing bigger to be seen. The giants were lying low, as is their custom.

I went stalking through the shallow's weed-bed, up to my waist in water. A carp swam within six feet of my toes! I was casting a little bit of cockle on to the surface weed, as close to fish as I could reasonably get without frightening them. But they weren't the slightest bit interested. Later, I tried with crust and this time interest was shown, though only by a few smaller fish.

About 4 p.m. I made myself a meal and would have had a sleep, only Ron and Roy came round for a chat and I ended up laughing at Ron's stories until the tears were running down my face. He has a superbly dead-pan delivery which makes the lunatic quality of his tales even more hilarious. And the funniest thing is that they're all true.

As the sun set I sat on the dam, float fishing. Suddenly I knew I should be on the island and went round there, taking the Hardy with me.

As I crossed the little bridge I saw a big cloud of bubbles, not thirty feet out. I stepped on to the island and saw a big common coming straight towards me. The rod still had a quill-float set 'lift' style but I dropped it straight under the rod tip and it lay flat in two feet of water. I could see the two beans on the hook, lying on the bottom. The common passed very close to the bait, and behind him, coming in from the direction of those bubbles, followed five more fish. Three of them were huge, between, say, 28 and 32. One of these, a mirror, saw the beans and went straight down. I saw her suck them in right below me. I waited a second as her gills puffed, then struck. The beans stayed in her mouth, the bare hook flew into the air! Slowly, she turned as I fell back against the tree, astonished. My movement, though not the strike (I'm sure), caused all six fish to bolt with a tremendous swirling and general disturbance of water. I was left staring at a cloud of mud, gradually settling as I watched.

What a dumbo! I'm sure it was my haste that lost me that fish. I was so sure she was going to eject the beans as she puffed her gills that I couldn't wait till she turned. But even so, it was bad luck. I was positive I'd connect. To miss seemed impossible.

As the light faded so I watched the white quill fade into the general gloom. When it was too dark to see I went back to the Stile, got down into my sleeping-bag and went straight to sleep. Clouds covered the moon.

Tuesday, 28th June - Newdigate Place

Fished in the Marsh Pitch, by the island. Baits were hurled out as far as the lily-bed thirty yards away. I had a pick-up from the bed on my left and that was a big fish. The line sizzled out, but he was coming towards me and when I struck, I missed! A big wave rocketed out. It was a finicky day. Lots of takes - then the wave as the fish powered off. I'd had three small wildies, then I had a fish that took the bait over to the left and I had to strike through a lot of bowing line. This one ran off to the edge of the island and was certainly the best fish of the day - but only 4½ lb - another wildie. I had one more; then as it seemed the big ones were still being finicky, I packed up - EARLY!

Friday, 1st July - Sheepwash

It was raining when I woke at 5.30. The wind was rushing at the leaves and it sounded stormy. Yet, even in my warm bed, I could feel it was a good morning for fishing. By 7.0 I was driving through the green and grey countryside. The sky was heavy and though the rain had stopped, it looked as if more was on the way. The trees swayed restlessly.

The wind was blowing down towards the shallows and I knew where I would fish. I dumped my gear at the Stump and tossed out a few handfuls of beans into the grey, broken water. But I didn't fish straight away. I went down to the shallows with the Hardy and some linseed, cooked just before I'd left (the beans had been cooked for the last Newdigate trip and they were far from fresh now, being soft and sweaty, though they still smelt acceptable . . . to someone who might live in a sewer!). Nothing happened at the shallows, save for a brief lift of the line. The rain fell again, then passed over. I crept back to the Stump and set up the Carpsticks. No. III was ready first and I cast two beans free-lined about thirty feet out. As I set the silver paper and rested it over some dead, wet leaves, I said to myself: "and before I could set up the second rod, the line was running from the first." I was convinced this would be a good morning; it was so like that morning in the Boathouse Pitch at Manor Pond, all those years before. I'd fizzled with confidence then and knew I'd get a good bag; these conditions were exactly the same - warm, breezy, drizzly and muggy - and I was almost delirious about it all.

As I baited up the hook on the second rod, so the silver paper rose on the first. I dropped everything and struck as the line began to peel off the spool. I connected fair and square and a fish charged steadily out, moving towards the trees. I crammed on sidestrain and managed to keep it clear of the dangerous, submerged branches. I pumped it gradually towards me and watched the turbulence appearing on the surface as the fish came under the rod point, but still deep down. Like my first carp of the season, I was convinced I was into a huge tench. The fight was so similar to the tussle of a green giant. The way that turbulence came up was like the disturbance from those big round fins and round tails. But it went round and round, with the rod hard over all the time, and when the net slid under it, it wasn't a tench at all but a long, lean mirror of 6 lb.

I cast again and then finished baiting up the second rod (C.S. II) and cast that one parallel to the bank, just out from the over-hanging trees.

After half an hour the silver paper on the first rod (C.S. III) twitched a couple of times, then rose up to the butt ring. As the line began to slide through, I turned in the pick-up and struck. There was a tremendous pull, and the clutch sang as the fish made a long run towards the lilies on the other bank. I only just managed to stop him reaching them. Then he turned left and ran powerfully up the lake towards the dead tree.

Immediately to my left was the alder that had given me trouble last year, when the line brushed and then caught in the branches. Already those branches were nearly touching the slanting line, even though I was reaching out as far as I dared. As the fish continued his slow run I put the rod top deep under the water and crammed on pressure to the limit.

For a minute or so the fish just kept boring and plunging, and though I wasn't giving it any line the rod was in a half-circle. I was worried in case it decided to make a run into my own bank, into the overhanging branches thirty feet away, but luckily when he did turn, he came back down the middle of the pool and so I waited till he was opposite me and then bent hard into him and gradually worked him in under the rod point. His head and mouth looked reasonably large but when I slipped the net under him and lifted him out I found he was another 'wild' mirror. A Sheepwash torpedo of 8 lb.

Half an hour later, the line again coiled off the spool and the strike connected with a fish that felt extremely solid. It didn't rush off anywhere, just lay deep, going round in slow circles and letting me bring it gradually in. With all the bushes and trees around I was expecting a sudden rush off to the right or left. This one felt like the wardrobe I'd been waiting for, but when I got it up to the surface it was only a 6 pounder - in spawn. That roundness of girth, so unlike a typical Sheepwash carp, had made it feel monstrous, even though it hadn't done much.

Never had I had more than two carp at a sitting at Sheepwash. But here were three and I cast expecting another and got it within forty minutes. 6³/₄ lb. Four! And all between 9 and 10.30 a.m.

At 11.0 the line ran out again. This fish surfaced about ten yards out but the line disappeared under the surface only five yards out! It was caught round some obstruction and for a while, as the fish see-sawed back and forth, I thought I would be lucky to get it. I brought it in towards me and just when I thought the carp was about to bang his head on whatever it was down there, he came free. He circled around for a bit, managing once more to get tangled up. This time in a small branch which he dragged around until I managed to fit all the mess into the landing net. Another mirror between 6 and 7.

The wind was still gusting down the lake. It seemed certain I would get another. But a patch of blue appeared above me and it began to brighten. For an hour nothing happened save for a short pull on the line. After one more hour I packed up, though I feel sure I would have had another if I'd stayed. Still; a record catch at Sheepwash and not one missed run. I got over to the Black Horse in plenty of time for lunch.

Sunday, 3rd July - Sheepwash and Newdigate

Woke as Guy came driving down the road to pull the centre-pin alarm system. *[Reel by my bed; end of line attached to a cardboard carp in the front garden.]* We had a cup of tea, packed up the bike and were away by 7.40 on a clear, still summer morning. The lanes were full of sweet smells and idiot birds (though I didn't hit any this time - birds that is!).

We got down to the lake to find the banks crowded! Bearing in mind the fact that this is meant to be *the* Golden Scale Club water, I think we should have a word to Mrs Charndley about allowance of 'a couple of the village lads'. It was like Brighton Pier. But, luckily, it didn't matter anyway. The carp were spawning. Poor Mem. He'd been there all night and hadn't had a touch. He said he thought it was coots fighting when it started. The shallows were loud with the carp as they pursued each other through the weeds and reeds. I climbed a tree to watch and to see if I could see any really big fish, but they were all about the same sort of weight as the ones I was catching last Friday - 5 to about 8 or 9 lb. There was only one fish that looked any bigger, certainly none as big as the one I saw three years ago.

"If they're not spawning at Newdigate," I said, "at least we'll catch a carp this morning. Let's go."

With Mem following on his bike, we wound back through the Sussex and the Surrey countryside. Being a Sunday morning I was amazed to find only one car in the members' car park. We'd have the pick of the swims after all. It was hot now, being 10.30, and a slight breeze was blowing up the lake, so we crept round to the inlet stream.

Fish were moving round the weed-bed and I had an 8 pounder first cast. I was expecting a good catch for all three of us, even though we only had a few hours to fish before various engagements called us home. We had plenty of takes but only one more carp - a little wildie which, unfortunately for Mem and Guy, fell to my rod. So they blanked at Newdigate, which is a fairly astounding achievement. (It will certainly be a mention-to-remember in dispatches.)

Thursday, 7th July

On this day of days I should have gone somewhere like Titmus where only on really lucky days are you in with a chance. However, I went early to a water where I couldn't fail - Newdigate. Still, I said to myself, as I rode through the green, sunny lanes, I might get a record for the water. I fished in the same place as last time, by the weed-beds in the corner, and before I'd had time to put the first rod in the rest, the line was slipping through my fingers. A 7 lb mirror came wallowing unsportingly to the net. A strong breeze began to blow, right past me and into the bridge end, where I had a good morning last year on a similar day - bright and hot but with plenty of cooling wind. So I switched to the bridge and after a few minutes had a fast run and hooked a fish which dived into the weed-bed but came out again after a tussle and then put up a good fight in the open water. $6\frac{1}{2}$ lb mirror. Again there were plenty of half-hearted takes that followed and plenty of runs that came to nothing. I landed another, smaller mirror. Broke on the strike (tut tut!!), lost one in the weeds and landed three wildies. The fish were still feeding well when I had to leave - the Racing Beans are still the favourite there.

Sunday, 10th July - Redmire

The drive from Clare's house (poor Clare, she was a bit down-hearted about my departure) was hot and humid. I left at 3 p.m.

and arrived at the pool just after 6.30. Old Mr Bufton was standing by his cottage as I drove up. I stopped to talk to him for a while. He looked like an old sepia photograph in his frayed brown suit and battered straw boater. Nearly a hundred years old and his eyes bright as a bird's. But he wasn't sure about the weather. "The storms are all round," he said, "but they always miss us."

Down on the banks of Redmire I had the place to myself. Big carp were moving up in the shallows, even though the breeze was blowing down to the dam.

As the sun began to set I cast out into the gaps in the weeds, under the willows, up by the shallows. Carp moved all round me. In the barley-field on the far hill, whitethroats kept up a ceaseless melodious chatter. It seemed a perfect evening. Still, warm; but the lines never moved, even though one of the two rods was the Hardy and the other the newly acquired Walker-built Avon[1].

Monday, 11th July

I woke in the '35' pitch, under the willows, dreaming that I was being pursued by swans. I'd set up stall there, with the rods dropped out in the margins, under the trailing branches. It was a cool dawn. The breeze was becoming a wind even though the day hadn't properly woken up. Fish were moving still. Every so often I heard a great splash as a big one turned over. The lines had not moved.

---

1. *This rod, a genuine Richard Walker MK IV Avon, built by him in 1954 or 5, was offered for exchange in* Angler's Mail *'Swap Shop'. The owner simply wanted any good glass 'tipster' rod. I bought him the best one on the market and still got the better bargain.*

After an hour or so I had a look around. There were bubblers off the Fence, but there were still carp to be seen in the shallows, right opposite my rods. Surely one of them would take a bean, the bait that had even cracked them at Sheepwash and which had nearly taken a monster off the island two weeks ago. The carp were interested then. But that was the first week of the season - Duffer's Week at Redmire. Things have changed since then - how much, I shall have to find out for myself.

By midday I was up the tree in the shallows, watching a big common nosing his way along. Yesterday evening I'd seen a 20 lb mirror picking up my free offerings - they were still interested in them, but not so interested that they were going to take one of the baited hooks.

I went to get the light tackle outfit - Mk IV Avon and 8 lb line - and climbed back up into the tree.

The big common was still there, with one or two others: all good fish. The common was huge - definitely 25 to 30, maybe more. The others were from around 16 to 22 (big doubles and little twenties!).

One of these fish went over the loose offerings I'd scattered and picked one or two of them up. Later, the big one also went down over them, but only once. A fish of around 20 lb swam into the line and bolted, taking the line with him. It tightened across his back until it came to the hook, which caught for a second. The clutch rang out and I thought I was going to mess the whole shallows up for the rest of the afternoon, but luckily the hook came free and after a brief look of uncertainty on all the other carp (the pricked one had disappeared) they settled down again and continued their slow progress round the shallows and through the weed-beds.

In a little while another good common carp came upon the hook-bait. His head went down and I took my eyes off him and watched the bow in the line. It began to straighten but dropped slack again. The fish swam slowly off, having somehow managed to snag me on an unseen obstruction. I bet he was laughing through his bubbles!

Nothing else happened in the tree, though another big common went straight under my perch and I couldn't get the bait down to him in time to intercept him. I left the Avon in the branches and took the Hardy on to Thistle Island. Big fish moved all around me but never quite came in range. They were all turning their flanks along the bottom, sending up clouds of red mud and flashing bronze coloured scales. I gave up and went to phone Clare and then have a drink and an amusing talk with Jack the Roadman, up at Langrove. He's a wonderful character, full of terrific stories and original country lore.

The sun was setting as I got back. After a light meal I went back under the willows in the shallows. There wasn't quite so much movement this time, though bubbles rose and fish humped in the weed-beds. Across the water, in the barley-field, the secretive whitethroats began their evening lullaby. The lines never moved, though this time I was using my 'BB' float on the Hardy and the tip stirred, just once.

Tuesday, 12th July

Float fished off the dam for a while. Nothing. The breeze was still blowing towards the dam but there was no hard evidence of feed-ing carp down that end - in fact there was no sign of carp at all.

I'd woken at 8.0 and the morning had looked promising. Dark, warm, even a few spots of rain. Opposite me the carp rolled in the thickest weed-beds. One came right out of the water and crashed back, upside down. Every twenty minutes or so a big fish leapt. I'd got no wandering instinct. I felt I was in the right place and had no urge to go hunting. One of the lines moved - Carpstick III - and a big ripple spread out where the bait had been cast. Twice more this happened - both on the same rod (8 lb line) - and each time my heart raced. But they came to nothing. Not even the silver paper moved. The carp were obviously interested, but not really hungry.

Still, by mid-afternoon, float fishing with the Hardy off the dam, I was far from despondent. In fact I was brimming over with glee at the thought of catching a Redmire carp in conditions that made them very elusive. The harder they are to catch, the more satisfying is the capture. And at a place like Redmire, I didn't mind waiting.

Roy arrived at 8.30, and though I was initially annoyed to have my solitude disturbed I was soon having an enjoyable conversation (released from my long silence).

A buzzard flew over as I strolled back to the Fence with a peanut-butter sandwich for my tea. It swooped suddenly at the edge of the wood and I leapt up on the bank to see if I could see any action. But I saw nothing. Coming back to my pitch I found Carpstick III had had another take - this time a few yards had been pulled and the beans had gone from the hook. Ah, well. I reeled in and once more began float fishing from the dam. After an hour, the orange quill sank quickly into the depths. But I missed the strike! The wind got up after I'd re-cast, but I reeled in when it became too dark to see the float and prepared to go back to the Fence for a sleep. But the bait had been taken. I re-baited with sweetcorn, cast again and after only five minutes had a slow run - which I missed! Again I cast, resting the rod on the dam rail and then lying back behind the tall grass out of the evening wind. Again the silver paper crept up to the butt ring and again I missed. Again I cast and within minutes, with my face right next to it, I watched the silver paper creeping from one ring to another. I waited this time till I could hear the faint hiss of the line, then struck gently (the bait was under the rod tip). This time

I connected; first blood to the Avon, though it was hardly a conspicuous christening for my new rod.

After a lively struggle, in came a hump-backed common of 6 lb. It had a very small tail, otherwise the fight could have been more fun on such light tackle. Still, big or small, I always feel better when I've caught my first carp - perhaps his grandfather will follow him to the net.

Wednesday, 13th July

Had an eel in the night. Woke late again, on a grey day. It was warm though and I thought some fish might be moving in the shallows. One or two carp were cruising around up there, but they didn't look 'prickly', they were just floating about.

I climbed the tree on the island and after a while, as I watched big carp moving about in the weeds below me, I suddenly spotted a monster moving with the others. As it moved, right below me, I was almost sure it was the Bishop, last seen in 1973, in my landing net. Perhaps my judgement was faulty, but that carp now looked as if it might weigh well over 40 lb. It also looked in tremendous fettle. I flicked a free bean out and it landed right in front of it (after dropping thirty feet). Dumbo took it on the drop! It was possible, I thought. Though thirty feet up an alder tree, it might be possible to hook and land a big fish, as long as I could get down through the branches to net it. I reckoned I could do it with or without assistance - and as Roy was still sound asleep it was going to be the latter. So I took the Avon up the tree and cast out the light tackle into a hole in the weeds only six feet from the carp. From my position, I could see everything clearly. I was sure that the fish would take the bait if only it found it in the dense weeds. He seemed to be picking up more loose offerings. He was moving into the right hole! But then he turned the wrong way, at the very last moment, and swam some twenty feet further out into the pool. I reeled up and took aim again. This cast would have to be accurate. I wanted the bait to land only a few inches from the fish. Now he was in more open water I thought there was even more of a chance, but the cast would have to be precise. I swung the rod, the tackle curved out and down and the 2 swanshot link landed right on his head! I had to sit down after that, in the branches. My polaroids had been steaming up with the tension, but now I was having a fit of laughter. Great cast Chris! The Bishop didn't come back.

I'd baited up a hole in the ruins of the old willow and after dark I took the Hardy round and flicked out a bait. Then I sat down in my little camp-chair and waited. Roy came round after an hour with a cup of tea and as it was getting a bit chilly I went back with him to his pitch to borrow a blanket. When I returned to my rod I found the silver paper in the butt ring! Curses! I should have got cold a few moments longer and just let Roy go back - I bet a carp knew we'd left the rod, in fact I'm sure.

I reeled up after another hour and got back into the Fence just as a heavy cloud let loose its load. As my kettle boiled, so the raindrops pattered down on my brolly.

Thursday, 14th July

Woke early, but all was quiet. The carp were not moving much even though the temperature was rising and the sky clearing. By midday it was quite hot and I wasn't reluctant to leave for Langrove and enjoy a cool pint with Roy. So far, Roy had nothing but an eel to show for his efforts, but I wasn't doing any better, considering I'd been fishing a day longer. If only the conditions would change. It was hot and the breeze was still easterly. What I wanted was a sharp south-westerly, a few heavy showers and then, come evening, a warm stillness. But the sky was pure blue and the hills were distant in the heat haze. The breeze was easterly and the carp weren't going to go mad. I bought some strawberries on the way back and had them for my tea, sitting back in the Fence and at least enjoying the serenity of it all.

Carp were beginning to move up to the shallows as the sun began to curve to the west. I moved up with them, sitting under the willow by the now fast diminishing weed-bed. The sun was right in my eyes and its reflection, too, was brilliant. Every now and then the reflection wobbled and broke. Carp were moving close to the beans I'd blow-piped out all over my side of the shallows. But though the evening was perfect, the air still and the willows lit with a golden light, the lines never moved.

After dark, I moved back to the Ruins and fished the hole under the branches. But in the clear air, the temperature was cooling very fast. By midnight, when I gave it up, I was shivering.

Friday, 15th July

I'd set my inner alarm clock to wake me at sunrise and sure enough, as I peeped out over the rim of my brolly, there was the sun, coming up yellow through the mist on the fields. I made some tea and then took the Hardy up into the shallows. But nothing moved in the misty water. I went though the willows round the top of the pool and came sneaking back along the western bank towards the islands. In the brambles was curled the same enormous grass snake I'd seen yesterday - well over five feet long. I saw nothing moving by the islands and so carried on down to the Ruins. No carp were bubbling out in the deep. Across the surface the swirling mists looked like a ballet of ghosts. The intertwining of the new warmth with the cold from the dawn caused eddies in the air, and here and there the mist went spiralling up in thin tubes, twelve feet and more tall. Roy woke up across the lake and thought I'd been by the willow roots all night long. It was nearly time to leave. The breeze began to stir the leaves - it was coming from the west! The carp began to point to the shallows. And I had to point back towards home.

Thursday, 21st July - Gatton Park

For the first time in history, I fished the Treetrap Lake legally! Roy had got me a ticket as a guest and at 3 p.m. I met him down on the bank, on the school side. He had already had a couple of wildies and I set up in an overgrown pitch next to his platform and soon I also had a couple of wildies, both on float-fished sweetcorn. But my position was too cramped, and with a fallen tree in front of me there was no finesse in my playing.

I moved to the far corner where a big chestnut overhangs the water and where there is an attractive-looking stretch of water between this tree and a patch of lilies.

As I came up to the water's edge, so I could see a carp right in the margins. I flicked him a bunch of sweetcorn on a size 6, and after a few seconds the line snaked out. The Hardy bent over and a tiny monster leapt out of the water, just like the sea-trout the rod was intended for (I could feel it smiling as it bent!). Another 3 lb wildie.

I cast the float out by the lilies (a float made from a piece of French corn stubble and only finished and varnished the day before) and cast free-line corn out under the chestnut branches.

The free-lined Hardy was first into a fish. But soon after, the corn stalk slowly sank from sight and the answering strike put a nice bend in the new Avon.

As the afternoon became evening, my tally rose to double figures. Already this was my best ever catch of carp. I'd never had more than five wildies before in a sitting, but here at Gatton they never stopped feeding. Just a few grains of corn every so often kept them in front of me and I didn't have to wait more than fifteen minutes before the stalk slid away, or the line tightened on the Hardy. I even changed tactics and hooked a tough fighter on crust from the middle of the pads. It took five minutes to beat!

One fish I hooked on the Avon ran twenty feet inside a second and then doubled back just as quickly. It only weighed $2\frac{1}{2}$ lb!

I got stuck on number 13 for half an hour. Then I got 14 and had a break for a few minutes. The sun was setting behind the woods on the far hill and the clouds were orange and grey. I got back to my fishing and once more the ripples ringed the dark corner of the pool and the Avon bent down to them. I netted number 16, then the centre-pin clicked and I struck and was into number 17. I had to net that one with another carp already in the mesh. The next one was the best one of the day. It certainly fought the hardest. Diving deep under the pads one moment, then racing into the branches the next. Twice I was forced to give line and the Hardy took on a glorious bend. Yet it was only $4\frac{1}{2}$ lb. A beautiful wildie. Perfect: long graceful form, like an aerofoil section, small scales, big tail. With eighteen such exquisite gems to remember I packed up, satisfied!

The owls were calling in the trees as we walked back up the grassy hill.

Monday, 25th July - Sheepwash

Showers had come over from the north-west during the day. By evening the sky was full of mountainous clouds, white, orange and blue-black. As soon as tea was finished, I cooked up some beans and drove to Sheepwash, along lanes wet with the rain, though the sky looked set to be fine for some time.

I'd thought that the shallows would be full of carp cavorting through the newly freshened water, their appetites tremendous. But there was hardly a ripple. True, there was some evidence of fishy presence - bubbles now and then or a quiet swirl - but nothing very enthusiastic. I didn't fish the shallows for long, but moved back to the Stump, remembering my success there three weeks ago.

Nothing moved on the surface. The moon grew brighter in the darkening sky. The screaming kids in the school on the hill were ordered to bed, thank God, and at least it was peaceful in the last hour. Very peaceful!

Thursday, 28th July - Newdigate Place

With the P's returned, Clare gone home, and the evening grey and damp after an afternoon downpour, I could only go fishing. Yesterday I'd ridden north of the local airport to buy one of the most beautiful rods ever made - the James Avocet. This evening, I wanted to christen it with a carp.

I arrived at the lake at about 7.30 p.m. and set up in the Marsh using the Avon, cast far out towards the lilies, and the Avocet flicked to the little lily-bed on my left. I was using a new departure from the paprika-flavoured beans - these new ones were coated in cinnamon!

Fishing had been slow, said Colin Brookwood (he and five other club members had only had one small carp between them and they'd been there since sunrise), but after the rain I was sure something was going to happen. I was just trying to work out why the thread had gone on my landing net attachment when there was a tremendous hiss from next to me. The line on the Avon was belting out. I trapped the line against the butt, waited a second, then swept the rod up. The tip bent hard over, and out between the lilies and the island a big swirl convinced me I'd hooked a mirror. The clutch was set a touch too loose and the carp easily made a long run into the island. I tightened up and swung him in, the Avon bent double. A good tussle ensued, close in. The fish kept down, swimming strongly from right to left, and every so often taking out a few yards of line. All the time the Avon was hard at work. Eventually, Colin netted it, a plump mirror of just under 7 lb. The other anglers were made slightly restive by my instant success. They had all begun to hate me. I re-cast both rods, putting the Avocet's bait out further this time.

The sun sank and lit the deep, grey clouds with a great wash of crimson. As it darkened, so all the other anglers on the lake packed up. Only I stayed, waiting, expectant. But it wasn't until another hour that the silver paper on the Avocet suddenly twitched. It twitched again, rising hesitantly, and I struck. The long rod was instantly alive!

This fish was no leviathan, though it still managed to dive into the lilies, and I had to slack off for a minute and then suddenly catch the little terror unawares and haul him out. A 2 lb wildie.

The clouds cleared and the moon showed bright and almost full.

Sunday, 31st July - Redmire

Arrived just as the sun was about to disappear behind the barley-field. The weed that I'd expected to clear during the past fortnight had, in fact, only half done so, but there was a great bed of it in the corner of the dam - dying weed that had drifted down the pool and had now packed itself tightly to about twenty yards from the overflow.

There were quite a few carp in that weed-bed; some basking, some cruising and some even pretending to spawn! I cast out from the little island, using aduki beans. Carp swam right over the baits, one fish even catching the line. But they weren't touched. As the moon began to rise behind and then above the wood, I set up my new brolly-camp, a little luxury that is really so much more practical than a car-cover and there's so much more room. Even if I do look like the stereotype carp-man, at least the rain and wind will never get me.

After I'd set up my pitch, in the Ash Grove, I took a couple of rods on to the dam and fished into the weeds from there. But I wasn't expecting anything and nothing happened.

I went for a walk along the far bank, looking at the moon, brilliant above the pool. The reflections were clear and still. I climbed the Island Tree and looked down on the black water. Water, sky - they were both the same colour; only the dam on the end of the lake interrupted the scene, like a bridge of trees arching into the night sky.

I walked back to the rods. Out in the bay a black shape came half out of the water and splashed back.

Monday, 1st August

Woke at dawn, but just for a brief look at the mist-shrouded water, the pale sky and the moon, still bright, over the dam.

I must have been tired as I didn't wake again till 10.0 and even then I felt a bit dopey. The silver paper on the nearest rod, rose slowly to the butt ring. I slid forward, struck, and the hook flew back into the trees behind me! Perhaps it was just a line-catch.

It was a hot day and the carp thought so too. I went for a walk after breakfast and there were dozens of big fish lying in the weed, right up near the dam. I thought it might be an idea to drop a bait in front of their noses. The first few just got fidgety, especially one that had the bait sliding down off the top of his head! Then a big mirror cruised into an opening just as the bait landed in front of him. He turned and the line began to slowly tighten. I struck and missed - *again!* I'm pretty sure the fish took the hook in as he seemed to go down after it. I should've waited.

It got so hot later on that I stripped off and dropped myself into the water from the island. I swam up right into the top of the shallows, pulled up a few snags, then swam back again. The water was like a bath up there, but colder under the trees. I sat on the bottom by the island with just my head poking out, looking along the surface for a carp. I didn't see any, so I got out and lay in the sun, watching a cumulus cloud forming out of thin air above me. It was as if an unseen aerial carp was feeding in heaven, sending up a puff of meteor dust as it grazed the blue sky. As it got dark I crept up to the shallows and fished from the platform. Carp were moving, but none liked my offerings. The moon rose over by the wood, a deep orange against the blue black. 10 p.m. and it was dark save for a glow in the west. I went back to the Grove and cast out kidney beans on two rods, then lay back and tried to sleep, but not successfully.

Tuesday, 2nd August

I wondered whether my sleeplessness was due to the fact that a fish was going to be caught. It's happened like that before; but this time I was not expecting anything and nothing happened.

One silver paper had moved a fraction and the kidney bean on that line was gone when I reeled up. I'd cast one bait over to the stump on the dam and then dropped it in, 'Walker' style, with a pinpoint showering of free offerings. But a lot of drift weed during the night had come up against the line and ruined any chance I may have had.

I wandered around, looking for feeding fish. It seemed there was a change in the air; for while it was still very hot, the clouds overhead, small and white, were blowing from the west. Gradually the breeze shifted until the ripples were, at last, going down to the shallows. From the Island Tree, I watched the carp turning to point that way, like weather vanes. Then they began to move forward, one by one. I followed, too, taking a couple of rods with me.

Nothing happened from the platform so I took the Hardy on to Thistle Island. A big common cruised right past me in the shallow water. I flicked out a bait and waited an hour. Other fish were moving; some came near, none liked the beans. I changed to sweetcorn and hooked a fish almost immediately. It wasn't big though, even though it did wrap me round a branch and get off!

I stalked a group of fish in the marsh, where the water is only inches deep. Some of them were big enough to please. The line tightened, I struck. A mirror. But only 7 or 8 lb. A perfect fish, though. Neat scaling with a tremendous humped back.

Two or three 20 lb commons were slowly promenading under the willows by the '35' pitch. I had one go down over my bait, but he obviously found it repulsive. In the end I gave up and went to phone Clare. I found her delightful.

The evening was calm, with a wet-looking sun low over the barley-field. I set up for a couple of hours in the willows again, sitting on a willow log. A few big fish were still moving - one came right up onto his tail and crashed back, making the shallows rock.

I was fishing with a kidney bean on one rod, and sweetcorn float fished on the Avocet. Was I being wise in offering a choice? Or just unsure. The float dithered and danced away. I struck and a big cloud of bubbles went hissing to the surface. The hook was fast in the overhanging willow! Two more good bites developed, both missed. I should have suspected the size 10 hook then and changed it for a Lion d'Or. I'd have been happier, later, if only I had done!

A big dark shape glided slowly over to the kidney bean. The line twitched, then fell slack. It was becoming overcast and the clouds brought the night in quietly. Following the rule of the wind, I'd set up further downwind - in the Fence. I cast out two rods, made a cup of tea, read a chapter on carp by F.J.T. (how keen becomes my appetite for fishing lit. when I'm up for a week at Redmire!) Then 'lights out'. I rolled up the front door so I could hear my s.p.s and went to sleep.

Wednesday, 3rd August

A bat flew into the line on Carpstick III and the erratic rustle had me out of my sleeping-bag in a moment. But in the dim light of the moon (and the first light in the east) I could see what had happened. The poor thing was fluttering around in the water, having caught round the line from the Avon as well. I brought him in and freed him, though I had to break the line on the Avon rather than try and untangle it from his wings. When I'd got everything sorted out I thought it might be an idea to put out the Avocet with some corn. This I did, casting it over to the right, free-lined as far as it would go.

The dawn was more distinct now, though the light was still grey and luminous, made stranger by the moonlight. I felt the urge for a cup of tea and was just about to light the stove when the hiss of silver paper had me back out over the rods. The Avocet! I struck immediately, though the run was smooth and steady and there was no rush. *[NO RUSH, he says - that was the first full-blooded hiss of silver paper I've heard this week!]* As the supple rod curved over, I had it in my head that this fish was only small. He ran out slow and deep and with every second that the clutch sounded, so he grew another inch! This was a good fish after all. He sailed out for a long way, cruising slowly to a heavy stop out towards the Stile. I kept a gentle pressure on (remembering the float) while I tipped the other rods into the water to keep their lines out of the way. I put the net in the water too, then I wound slowly down and bent into my adversary. For a moment or two nothing happened and I had a sudden panic in case this fish had weeded itself with such a tiny hook. But he was just lying doggo and in a few seconds he began to move. He came in ten yards, then made another reel-screaming run. I kept the pressure light and he slowed and then turned, making a slant towards Bowskill's Tree. For a time I just kept a steady bend in the rod, then, as it seemed he wasn't going to stop, though he was only going very slowly, I bent the rod harder. Still he continued. There was something under that tree he wanted to get to and as I didn't know what it was, whether just some weed and overhanging branches or perhaps a big snag I hadn't noticed before, I would have to stop him. The long rod arched right over. He wasn't slowing. Then: 'ping'! There was a jerk, then a big bow wave shooting back out into the lake and the line hanging slack. The blasted puny hook had pulled! I suppose I've used smaller than 10 before for large carp. But this one was a Sundridge. Yurgh! I ripped it off the line and flung it away.

How big? In the half light I never got a clear view, I'll only say it was big and leave it at that.

Needless to say, out went all rods on corn. I had one more run before 7 a.m. Again on the Avocet. I struck and impaled two scales. The fish was three years old; thank goodness. *[But wait a moment; at 10 lb a year maximum growth rate, that carp could have been . . . Aw shudup.]*

A gentle breeze began to blow and the sky looked grey, though there was blue sky behind me. Would it rain? Grey and dark grey layers came in over the barley-field, but they didn't seem to be building. I suddenly thought I should go round to the Stile. Fish were bubbling there, but though I put two rods out nothing happened.

Up in the shallows were the usual small number of big commons. I cast out and in a while a dark shape went up to one of the baits. The line tightened. I was going to strike. But then it fell slack and the fish cruised off. This happened again, with another, bigger fish. I feel sure they mouthed the baits and then felt the check of the link. Perhaps a lightning strike . . . but I didn't get another chance.

The wind began to veer crazily. One minute it was blowing up into the shallows, the next it was gusting into the dam. The fish moved with it.

The sky cleared of cloud even though a few spots of rain had fallen earlier. I found out later that Hereford had a downpour, only a few miles north-west. But by midday, the sun was blazing again and I went into Langarren to buy a choc-ice and order half a dozen homemade bread rolls. When I got back I felt sure I'd get a fish, floating some cat biscuits off the dam. But the baits just bobbed in the incoming ripples, causing maximum uninterest.

Big carp had moved back into the pack-weed at both corners of the dam. Some of them I recognised and they were in exactly the same places as I'd seen them on Monday and Tuesday. It was a precise formation that they only maintained during those particular conditions. Highly mysterious.

Over by the outlet, I suddenly spotted an enormous carp at the far side of the weeds. There were a lot of 20s lying in the middle of the bed, but this fish, further out, dwarfed them all. It wasn't the '38'. It was much darker on the flank, possibly a common, though I couldn't see that clearly. It was much much bigger than the '38' too. It turned head on. It was unbelievable. I don't think it was anywhere near as big as the King, the Redmire Monster, but it was definitely way over the record. It was just basking and I didn't even try and cast out. (Should I?) I went to get my rolls, still hot from the oven, and when I came back the wind was changing again. This time it was following the direction of the clouds, blowing hard across to the east bank.

From the weed-filter, I had a slow dip and draw on the 'BB' float. The culprit was a little scamp of a common (I would have liked to have taken him home).

The wind increased to a near gale, blowing right into my pitch in the Fence. I gathered my things and went back there to take my tea, while the baits lay in the choppy water where, I felt sure, there were dozens of equally hungry fish. But I was wrong, again. The sun is now behind a yellow, wet-looking strip of cloud as I write. Soon it will set. Above that cloud bank there are high, wispy cirrus clouds raked by stormy winds. Here, by the water's edge, the surface is now calm. But the air has a chill to it that seems to smell of rain. The sky says the same. I have to leave soon. If the rain falls in the next twelve hours I'm in with a chance. Gulls are coming in from the direction of the clouds, from the west. As they pass, high overhead, I'm hoping the storm is not far behind.

Thursday, 4th August

Slept late (too many early dawns!) and when I woke, the wind was up. There was cloud, but too much blue sky. I could see the heavier rain clouds just peeping over the Welsh hills, but they weren't coming my way.

Up in the shallows, the ripples were the size of waves and I thought there must be dozens of fish up there. But from the tree I could only see a couple of faint mud clouds coming up - the wind had whipped up the bottom silt and the shallows were cloudy anyway; only by watching for the odd, furling billow could I detect where the carp were.

I fished there all morning, but nothing happened. Nothing happened all day, except that as the wind became stronger, I was convinced it would bring rain over and so I decided not to leave at 4 p.m., as arranged, but stay on one more night and leave the next morning. Phoned home to tell Nick and he said he'd had a 15 pounder from Lodge - which was a somewhat better catch than mine.

After the sun had set, yellow and wet-looking, I sneaked up into the shallows again. From the tree I saw an enormous fish swirl. And there were others, coming in right beneath me. I got the rods and cast out a Kidney Bean on one and a Racing Bean on the other. Within minutes I had a slow run on the K.B. but it was a line pick-up. A big swirl broke through the ripples. Later I had a slow run on the K.B. I'm not sure whether this was a real pick-up or not - I missed! Nothing more. The wind roared at the willow on the other side. All round me the branches shook furiously. There was to be no calm this evening.

At 10.30 I gave up fishing and crawled back into the peace of my bivouac, where I could hear myself think. I made a cup of tea, while the night went wild outside.

Friday, 5th August

Woke to the sound of RAIN! Just a few drops, then silence (except for the odd rush of wind), then a great downpour. It was still dark and I fell asleep, smiling.

When I woke, at 6 a.m., it had stopped. The lake looked perfect and I quickly cast all rods. A fine drizzle began to fall. A few strings of bubbles rose. What more could I ask? Just one carp, perhaps? Please?

Wednesday, 24th August - Redmire

Left home later than I'd planned but as it turned out, I was pleased I did. It poured continually for the first one hundred miles of the journey. At Brize Norton there was a spectacular break in the clouds on the western horizon and by Ross the sky had lifted and the rain stopped.

I set up in the Ruins and as I did so the clouds broke up slightly. A strong breeze was blowing down to the shallows and I suppose, really, I was at the wrong end of the pool. But I'd made up my mind and now here I was, setting up two rods with 7 lb b.s. casts attached to 10 lb b.s. lines (Nick had got some 7 lb Stark at lunchtime; and now the weed had died back, I felt far more confident using lines as light as I dare go).

It seemed I'd only just cast out (both baits sweetcorn) when it got dark. Roy, a little damp as he'd got here at 1.0, came inside my camp for a cup of tea and I was just about to open a bottle of

milk when, above the faint rush of wind in the trees around us, I
heard a steady hiss.

I burst out of the candlelight into the darkness to find the line
on C.S. III belting out. I struck and connected. But though the
clutch rang out, the carp wasn't more than 5 lb. A fat little common. I thought perhaps a bigger fish might follow, but nothing
happened until midnight, when I fell asleep.

Thursday, 25th August

Woke to the sound of torrential rain hammering over my head.
Dry and warm, I went back to sleep.

By 10 a.m. it had stopped though only long enough for me to
bait up with black gramms, blow-pipe a pound out into the water
and then quickly retire as another black cloud dropped its load
over Redmire.

I felt sure of success. The rain and the wind. Perfect conditions,
as long as the rain stopped for a while. But it never really stopped
for long enough. It's quite pathetic how I'm always yearning for
perfect weather.

Towards evening, the sky at last began to break up. The sun shone
over a glistening, soaking landscape. I went up to the shallows with
the Hardy but couldn't see a fish to cast to, though I fancied the
look of the willow on the other bank. But before going round there,
I walked up to the barns and then beyond the brow of the hill that
overlooks Redmire. Looking west, where the sun was curving, was
a beautiful scene of small hedged-in fields, woods and high hills.
On the furthest horizon were the dark banks of the Black Mountains, their tops almost touching the swiftly moving clouds.

Back at the waterside, I threw out a handful of corn, just

beyond the submerged willow shoots that grow out of the water under the sweeping branches of the parent tree. I flicked out the little cork-bodied quill and remained standing, holding the rod. If I'd sat down the sun would've been directly in my eyes. But anyway, I was tense with expectancy. I knew I would hook a carp.

A small mirror appeared right at my feet, burrowing his nose into the mud. I glanced back at the float and it was turning in a circle. But I'd missed it. I left it alone and after a few minutes, it slid through the ripples (the wind was still steady), settled, turned, then moved quickly away across the surface. I struck and a large fish shot into the sunken branches to the right. The centre-pin screamed just once, then the line fell slack and a tremendous swirl broke the surface as the carp turned and then shot out into the open water. Grattz! The hook had slipped. I re-cast and in fifteen minutes the float again slid under and I struck into a fierce, though juvenile, fighter around 6 lb (he made a tremendous dive into the sunken willow).

On the next cast the float didn't have time to settle before it disappeared. The carp must have taken the corn on the drop. Again I had a good tussle, though I knew almost immediately this was no big fish. The reel screeched and the shallows were cut with sudden, arrowing ripples. A 5 lb common. There were no more bites after that. The sun had set and I walked back around the lake to my bed. The moon was bright over the wood.

Friday, 26th August

So quickly! I seem hardly to have arrived.

The sun was bright when I woke. I baited up the pitch again with black gramms and cast both carp rods. Just after breakfast, there was a hesitant pull on the right-hand rod. No other response.

I re-cast and went for a quick look in the shallows. When I returned, the silver paper was again up. Damn! I cast again. An hour later there was another, slower pull. I struck on this one, but there was no connection.

I had my luncheon, then went round to the shallows. There was nothing to be seen under the willow, but on the other side of the sunken willow I found plenty of carp. Out went the quill, next to the trailing branches. But for an hour it never moved, though carp passed close by . . .

I began to feel sleepy. Perhaps it was the sun, or the meal, or the wine. Anyway, I dozed for a while, half dreaming. Then I sat up and noticed a couple of carp close in, under the branches. I dropped the quill in there and within seconds, it slowly turned and sank. I struck and a fish immediately dived straight under the tree. The centre-pin screeched as the fish forced its way further and further through the submerged branches. The Hardy bent double. The carp thrashed and splashed. I'd stopped him and now he was beginning to come back. Slowly, with the rod hard over all the time, I managed to persuade him from his sanctuary. Then, suddenly, he was clear of the branches and the quill showed again, much to my relief. But the fight was far from over. The fish lunged straight out, then turned left, back with the willow. But he was held back by the line catching against the barrier of shoots just there and I swung him back.

Roy was coming round with the net, for although this was nothing special, the fish looked over 10 lb in the water. He certainly sounded it! Plunging and splashing around. The net was pushed out over the weeds and branches and I heaved him gently into the mesh. 10 lb exactly, on Roy's scales, though mine said lighter. A perfect, if small, Redmire carp 'sat' for his portrait. And another excuse for another pot of tea. Roy even produced a splendid cake that he'd had squirrelled away all this time.

An hour later, I went back to the willow and Roy came round too, fishing the other side of the tree, where I'd hooked the big fish yesterday. Like me, he was float fishing and in the first half an hour we both had deliberate takes, my quill sliding across the surface, which we both missed.

The sun was behind the bushes on the other side of the shallows. A chill air was coming, gently, from the fields behind me. I was sitting back against the old willow-trunk and every so often a deep drone sounded from somewhere within the maze of cracks and niches. It sounded as if the tree was sleeping.

A big, dark shape, cruised slowly past my float - a 20 lb common. A patch of bubbles rose. I reeled in, re-baited with two fresh grains of corn and cast out again. But the quill curved too much to the left and the line was hanging from a branch. Never mind, if I tried to retrieve it I'd probably get caught up and lose my float, if I left it and hooked a carp I was positive it would come free.

Minutes later the float moved. Very slowly it turned and came towards me, then turned again until it was sliding confidently away. I struck, and the reel sang out. The carp went straight for the nearest snag and the tight line sprang from the overhanging branch with no trouble at all. The snag was a willow shoot, but the fish just knocked it flat and the line failed to catch round it. Roy came round as my opponent made a long, safe run away from the snags and into open water.

"He's not big," I said, "the same as the last one; but he's certainly a fighter!"

The little rod arched round as I turned the carp over in the water. He swung to the left, then to the right. If he had kited I would have been in trouble, but he obligingly kept a tight line. I worked him slowly in but he wouldn't go round the sunk trunk and insisted on coming in the awkward side. With a last flurry, he was in the net. 9 lb of glistening common, slightly different in shape from the last one, but definitely the same generation.

It's curious, but I've had far bigger fish - twenties - from Redmire, that haven't fought nearly as well as those last two, young commons. What they lack in long, heavy pulls, they make up in fantastic speed and sudden, surprise changes in direction. Where snags abound, the odds are in their favour.

Roy returned to the Stile, where he's been all week; I went back under the trees by the old willow stump, cast out the rods and turned in for the night.

The sun was glowing through light cloud when I awoke. I 'piped' out another pound of black grains and re-cast my rods. The baiting of the hooks was a real chore with such tiny, hard, brittle bait. After three days of it I was now getting impatient and careless rather than quick and proficient.

At 11.30, as I was preparing to 'pipe' out another load of grains, the silver paper on the Avon, rose from its rest in a brown paper bag and hissed steadily. A REAL RUN! I struck and the rod wound into a tight half-circle. A heavy fish moved steadily right. For five seconds there was as much tension in me as the rod. Then, as the rod flicked up and straight, I was left straining at nothing at all, just a limp line. I could have hurled my rod right across the pool when I reeled in and found a hard little grain over the point of the hook.

Later on, as I was float fishing off the dam - the breeze having turned towards that direction - I had an exquisite slow, sinking take just as Roy was trudging (quietly) past me with a load of gear. He was packing up and loading his car, as cheerful and good humoured as ever, even though he'd not even hooked a fish all week. So I struck, and immediately thrust the bending rod into Roy's free hand. He dropped the bag from his other hand, got a grip on the situation, and joyfully played in a Redmire rocket of about 8 lb. He would have gone home happy anyway, but now he'd had a carp to add to his memories.

Thursday, 8th September - Lodge Pond

It began to rain as Nick and I drove through the grey and green towards Farnham. It was warm, almost muggy. A perfect, late summer day for carp. The rain was too much to begin with and we spent the first hour not fishing but drinking and eating at the Ghost Man's pub at Bentley. When we got to the water, Rick had already arrived and was waiting impatiently on the bank.

"They're bubbling like mad!" he said.

We put out two rods each. Baits were the proven Racing Beans (first success was here at Lodge) and my new discovery - Kala Chana - or yellow gramms. But for two hours, though carp were moving and bubbling all round us, not a line moved. Rick discovered enthusiastic bubbling a few yards further down towards the deeps. After a while we both moved up to the bulrush beds where carp were feeding only a little way out. I'd set up the Hardy with a quill. It moved, just after a shower of rain, but there wasn't enough to strike at. Bubbles were surfacing everywhere. I just had to go and get another rod. Out it went. After a few minutes, a fish picked up my bait and the reel screeched, but I was watering a bush, and the carp had departed before I could get back to it. I concentrated and watched the lines tightening twice - once good enough to strike at - both came to nothing. Rick had a run. I heard the rattle of his silver paper and then saw a big bow wave go out from the margins. He'd missed the bounder.

I had a look up the bank, back towards my original pitch and I found an area where the truffling was almost furious. Confident though I was, in my tricky pitch behind the bulrushes, I just had to move and cast out towards those great patches of sizzling bubbles and slightly rippling water. The sun, that had broken through the grey, now shone out bright and orange, low on the horizon. It came behind a tree on the far bank. I cast the Hardy as far as I could (not far - thirty feet perhaps), saying to myself, "A Hardy never lets you down!" I tossed a few gramms around the float, then went for a sneak back to my original pitch, just to see what was happening. There were a few patches of bubbles, but nothing tremendous. The lake was calm now, just before sunset. The only disturbance to the surface was the movement of fish and the breaking bubbles.

'Reeek!' 'Reeeeeeek!' The centre-pin. The Hardy! I began to run. Rick was running too. I got there first. The carp had run thirty yards and as I picked the rod out of the rushes a big swirl opened up in the middle of the lake. There was a violent pull and the reel screamed again. The fish rolled and swirled. Other carp bolted away from the disturbance. I moved along the bank, to the next opening in the rushes to the left. From there I began to slowly work the fish in towards me. Rick prepared the net. The sensation on the line made me quite optimistic. It plunged and splashed, but never got its head down. I got it in front of us and kept the pressure on as I worked it through the rushes. It didn't want to come. It somersaulted lazily out and then somersaulted back again. Rick reached out as I heaved it half over the mesh. He lifted as I pulled again and luckily the carp, that we could now see was a good one, didn't bolt. I'd said he was at least 40 lb and as Rick swung him ashore I knew he was the biggest I'd taken from the Lodge. First for the yellow gramms, too. Actually, it wasn't 40 lb. It was 14 lb. (I have to have a little dream sometimes.)

A mist began to creep out from the trees. The sky was clear and the evening became almost cold. As it grew dark, we packed up, my fish being the only one caught. Nick had insisted on staying up in the furthest shallows and I reckon he would have had something if he'd moved down with us. But fish or no fish, he was content with his day. I was content with the fish and the day.

As we drove home, Nick said how much this day reminded him of his misspent youth and especially of all those other misty Septembers when he could go fishing whenever he pleased. I almost told him he wouldn't be sounding so nostalgic and regretful if only he hadn't got himself a regular job. But I offered to buy him a pint instead.

Monday, 12th September - 5th Session at Redmire

'On the 12th of September, Roy and I went again to Redmire.'

It was twenty-five years to the day since Walker had set off on the eve of his record catch. As we drove as fast as the old van would go, through the warm, sunny afternoon, I wondered if the omens were right. So far, so good, I thought. My picture for the publishers had been accepted that morning, giving me my freedom for the rest of the week. I'd discovered a new bait. It was the eve of the new moon.

We arrived at Bernithan just as a red sun touched the Welsh mountains. A breeze was rippling the waters of Redmire in towards the dam. I wanted to fish the Willow - 'Walker's Pitch'. So did Roy. We tossed; I won.

It was nearly dark by the time I'd cast out. Three rods baited with yellow gramms. I folded large tubes of silver paper over the lines, then sat back to watch for shooting stars. I saw none.

I made some tea. Read a bit of *Drop me a Line* then went to sleep at around 11.30. Big carp had been rolling since darkness fell but with the sudden, intense chill, I hadn't been too optimistic.

Tuesday, 13th September

Woke out of a deep, dream-filled sleep, to the rush of silver paper. I burst from under the canvas into the sunlit dawn and there was the sight of sights. The silver paper vibrating at the butt ring and the line streaming from the open spool. I snapped in the pick-up on C.S. II and struck. A great weight surged from left to right, and out under the mist I saw a big wave open out, heading for the dam. After ten yards the first run came to a solid halt and I felt the uncomfortable sensation of the tight line squeezing through a mass of weed. The rod top trembled with the vibration. Everything had jammed too abruptly and I felt like a pilot who'd lost control at a crucial moment.

Suddenly, the fish thumped. The line creaked. He thumped again, very hard, and rushed off to the left. The mass of weed couldn't keep up with him and the line snapped at the hook. I reeled in perhaps twenty pounds of weed, all quite green and fresh.

The sun shone its beams through the mist. It could have been such a perfect dawn. As it was, I'd lost my appreciation of the surroundings and went off to strangle a fence post.

I made some tea, had some breakfast, and prepared the Hardy. Roy came round and I told him the sad news. He began float fishing off the dam and after a while hooked a small common. I had a run on the Hardy, but missed.

The sun rose bright and warm. I had another run on the Hardy and this time connected with a spirited mirror of 6 lb.

A big, dark shape cruised past, not far out. The sun had brought the monsters out. Up in the shallows were one or two good fish, along with a number of small ones. From the platform, I cast float tackle and a grain of corn and watched with amazement as a big carp came out of the willow on the far side of the shallows and swam straight over, for twenty yards, towards the float. It bobbed as the carp sucked at the bait; but just as I was going to strike, he turned slowly away and swam off. Immediately, as if satisfied by the big brother's 'test', a smaller carp took the bait and the float slid under. It fought superbly for such a diminutive specimen but I soon swung him in and lifted him out by hand. 5 lb. From the tiny island I hooked another, only slightly larger fish. This got off after a tussle. The sun was curving into the west and both Roy and I left the shallows and went back to the deeps.

I re-cast the rods from the Willow Pitch again, set the papers and, after a bit, went to see how Roy was faring, float fishing from the dam.

The sun was almost on the line of the edge of the valley. Our shadows were long. We could only have been talking for a minute when I heard a rattling coming from the direction of my pitch. For a second I stood still, then leapt back across the dam, over the stile and up to the rods. The line on C.S. III was streaming out. I struck and a big wave went shooting off to the right, in the same direction as the morning fish.

"I'll need your help with this one!" I shouted to Roy, who stood watching from the dam.

The fish had stopped for a moment. I bent the rod harder and the line jagged back. For a second I thought he might have just shot towards me, like another big fish I remembered. But I hadn't my lucky star with me this time. In came a load of weed and suddenly a huge whelming bulge appeared on the surface, as carp and man disengaged. A gigantic wave went back up the lake, arrowing away at a steady speed like a phantom powerboat until it was lost from sight behind the leaning trees.

Had the line gone again? No. There was the hook. And there were the two gramms of Kala Chana! I'd not noticed how badly cooked - or rather, uncooked - they were and so, in my haste to get away the previous morning, I had only boiled them for twenty and not thirty minutes, like I should've done, and although I was careful with my baiting-up, I was not careful enough. Thus another fish-of-the-season, or maybe fish-of-a-lifetime, was stupidly lost.

To my amazement, I had yet another full-blooded run. This time, just after midnight on a cold, bright starlit night. It was on the Avon and I burst out of my sleep, rolling on to my knees behind the rod, with the foil quivering at the butt ring, glowing with a strange grey light. I struck and a great weight almost pulled the rod top into the water before the clutch sang out. This fish headed left, away from the dam and it felt, like the previous two, huge. But again the rod sprang back and I was left staring up at the Milky Way, a great emptiness in me. The bait was still on the hook.

Twenty-five years previously, Dick Walker was probably lying in the same place that I was, comatose after a day spent celebrating his momentous catch. I just gazed up at the stars, wondering why I should have suffered such a day of momentous bad luck.

At sunrise, Roy, fishing opposite in the overspill corner, made up for all the disasters and landed an absolutely magnificent common of 26 ½. It took a bunch of tares on a size 10 and is Roy's biggest carp ever. So at least one of us got a fish of a lifetime.

Wednesday, 21st September - Newdigate Place

It was a dull, cold morning. But I wanted to go fishing, even though there were photographs I should've been taking. I wanted to find out if the yellow gramms would go well at Newdigate and most of all, I wanted to catch a carp.

By midday I'd cast two rods. The Avon took a turn with the centre-pin and float, cast to the hot spot at the edge of the little lily-bed in the Swamp Pitch, and C.S. III cast out the furthest bait towards the large lily-bed thirty yards away. I scattered a pint of gramms over the water and sat back on a sack to wait. It was not until after 1.0 that the line on the furthest cast slid out a few inches. Perhaps they were suspicious of the gramms. They did look a little like the Racing Beans. The Newdigate carp had seen enough of those now, even though I was the only angler (up to last month) who had been using them.

The silver paper was still. Yet in the grey light I could just see the unmistakable signs that the bait was working, and working as well as that first, memorable day I used the Racing Beans - almost exactly a year ago. Great billows of mud came furling to the surface. All over the baited area there were silent, brown clouds rising, then diluting into a general discoloration of the water. And all that for no more than a pint of Kala Chana - well scattered too.

The orange-tipped quill, over to the left, without any suddenness slid to the right and under. Had it moved slightly just before? A slight movement that caught my eye and made me concentrate? I reached over for the Avon and struck. A biggish wave convinced me I was into a mirror. The rod bent double as it took the strain of the first run, not into the lilies, but out towards the island. The centre-pin gave out its battle-cry! On the 7 lb cast I couldn't be too severe, but the fish was soon rolling on the top and changing his direction for a new haven: the weed-bed twenty yards to my right. He nearly got in too. I coaxed him towards me and knew he wasn't going to embarrass me, but he was a spirited fish and it was a long time before I got him coming over the net. He made one more long run, the Avon throbbing and bending, then I got him to dive in the net first time. There was plenty of fight left in him even then, and he thrashed about in the mesh. 9 lb 14 oz - the biggest from Newdigate so far and, I think, the biggest caught by any member this year - a good test for the newly spliced Avon. I was pleased that it handled perfectly. (Last week it had been run over by a Hoover and had its tip fractured!)

I lowered the carp back, washing the bits of leaves off his flanks, that were already beginning to turn their autumn orange. Then he wrenched himself out of my hands and bolted.

I stood up and thought I could hear the 'hypnotic hiss'. I could. The silver paper on C.S. III was jammed at the butt ring. I trapped the line, waited a second, then struck and a wildie came thrashing from the island.

At 2.15 the silver paper again shot to the butt ring. It was an incredibly fast run, impossible to miss.

On the light line (4 lb) this wasn't going to be easy. It was a good fish, heading straight for the island. Somehow, I turned it, and it swung round, gave a few yards of line, then rushed off to the lily-bed over to the right and out. The Altex buzzed. I just hung on and managed to pull the carp a few inches further to the right of his target. By the time he had reached it, the inches had become feet and he missed the lilies by a yard. Then I applied an ounce more pressure and the line went, right down at the hook. It was so sudden I thought perhaps the teeth had done it. It looked that way, and I wasn't applying the full 4 lb. Pity, as it might have been a big wildie - and I'd have been well pleased to get one of the real big ones - though I've got a feeling it was another goodish mirror. Ah well! I had another run on the carp rod which I savoured for a few seconds and marvelled at the way the line went hissing through the foil. Then I struck, and in came a wildie that must have weighed 1 ½ lb. I packed up then. Not bad, though. Four fish in three hours. All bodes well for the bait that no one - not anyone - will discover. Heh, heh!

Friday, 23rd September - Newdigate

The film was at the processors so, while it was being done, I was going fishing.

I was too late getting up though and it wasn't until noon that five handfuls of grains had been thrown out and the rods cast. They were all cane this time - the Avon out furthest, the Avocet with the Altex, and the Hardy back with the centre-pin. But as that third rod might cause complications I only had a couple of casts with it. Two rods is bad enough. Forty-five minutes after casting and only seconds after I'd tossed in a few more grains, I had a nice paced run on the Avocet. I had just been beginning to wonder if the Swamp was the right choice, as the wind was at my back and no mud clouds were visible in the baited area.

On the light tackle, I kept things quiet for a while. The carp stayed low and fairly slow and I was pretty sure I was into a mirror, but after a few minutes of grovelling around on the bottom, I applied a bit of pressure and saw I'd only got a small wildie. I hoisted him straight out over the net. 3 $\frac{1}{2}$ lb.

Ten minutes later, the silver paper on the Avon, still for an hour, rose smartly up to the butt ring and quivered there as the line flickered through. I trapped the line against the butt, hesitated for a second as it tightened, then struck. The rod wound over as a big-feeling fish swayed on the end of the long line. I should have really hauled then, even though the line was only 7 lb b.s. The carp wasn't yet under way and I had an early opportunity to gain a few yards on him. But then he dived away, past the pads and out past the island channel. The clutch might have been a little tighter, as it was it screamed out intermittently. The fish rolled and gave ground, and instead of pumping I walked backwards up the long bank. He turned and charged out again, passing the lily-bed once more, but this time veering left, heading for the same place where I lost my biggest Newdigate carp a year ago. I piled on the sidestrain and he rolled only six feet from the edge of the snags. I coaxed him back, thinking he must hit the edge of the island and, as I wound, seeing the rod straightening out a little. He was coming in. I should have run backwards once more, but before I could think, the carp surged away again - a long screaming run between the dangerous 'jaws' of island on left and lily-bed on right.

This was the toughest scrap I'd ever had at Newdigate. I was giving the tackle all the stick it could take, yet I couldn't get that carp to come in further than the near edge of the lily-bed. So far he'd played all his cards for the island stakes, ignoring the nearer prize of those tough green stems. Just as I was beginning to think I might swing him my way, he made a sudden lunge to my right - heading for those pads! I lay the rod over, piling on side-strain. He was slowing. He was almost there though, and the big wave had practically reached the line-trap. And then it was all over. The line was slack. I reeled in quickly, horrified in case I'd given too much pressure at the crucial moment. But there was the hook, skipping across the water just behind the link. But, like a fool, I'd forgotten to bend out the exaggerated offset in the point. That was a tip Tom had given me on Monday. I'd remembered to do it on all the hooks, but not this one. Bloody idiot!

It's always hard to estimate the size of a lost fish. But I've had a lot of carp now from Newdigate and never have I felt anything like that one. Perhaps it was a really big wildie, but I reckon it was a double figure mirror. I punched a tree. I cast again but I never had another touch on that line. One more run came to the Avocet, a wildie of 1 lb!

Monday, 26th September - Newdigate

Decided to fish for a longer, more serious session. Nick caught me before I'd got two miles though, and by the time we'd talked, had a pint and parted, it was 1.30 p.m. But it didn't make any difference, anyway. For some reason, though the day was warm and bright, the carp never got their heads down. There was no discolouring over the baits. There were a few short, sharp runs. One I hit - a small wildie. I had two small tench on float tackle. I was just moving pitches when a big fish ran on the Avon. I had my watch in my hands and I fumbled the strike and missed.

I fished the day out on the opposite side of the lake - the Picnic Pitch. The water looked better there, but the 'far-off' rod hardly had a sniff. The Hardy, with the float, did better; close in, by the lilies. First cast, the quill dipped and a big fish bolted. And again. Then I cast right over the little bed. After a few minutes, it bounced under. Another big wave went off in a panic. But then it slid under again and this time the line followed. I struck, and after a fine fight on the light tackle, having to bring the carp right through the middle of the lilies, I landed a 3 lb wildie.

The sun had set and now the full moon rose over the trees opposite. A heron shouted across the silence and made me jump. I'd taken the quill off the Hardy and was fishing free-line. The silver paper hissed, I struck and missed!

Then three moronic poachers arrived with a bloody tilley lamp and so it was time to go. I should have gone to Sheepwash.

Wednesday, 28th September - Sheepwash

Conditions today were almost the same as on July 1st, when I had my record catch. It was mild, windy and dark, with spots of rain now and then. I fished the same pitch as July too - only this time I was using yellow gramms. Apart from a slow lift of one silver paper, nothing happened. I didn't see any signs of carp for all the four hours I fished. However, the farmer's pretty daughter did come all across the fields just to give me a mug of tea. Very welcome she, I mean it, was too.

Monday, 3rd October - Redmire

As usual, left far too late. I had to go to London in the morning to deliver some work to Michael Joseph - luckily, it went down well (one of the two pictures was a photo of a big Redmire carp) and I could set off with a clean slate (almost). But by the time I'd said goodbye to Clare (compulsory), had a good dinner (essential) and got the van loaded, it was past 3 p.m. I didn't get to the pool until dark.

A wind howled all night. The roar of it in the black poplars kept waking me up as I lay, warm, in the Fence. It was very warm. Warmer than the first nights of June.

The sun was bright in the morning, but the wind kept up. Not a touch on the three rods so, after a few hours, I took the Hardy and went for a wander up the shallows. There was nothing on my side, but I climbed a tree on the west bank and saw a fair-sized common feeding, right beneath me. Then I went up the Island Tree and there they were. A good number of big carp, moving around beneath the ripples. I went back for the Hardy and the Avon and fished from the platform. There were one or two small carp feeding not far out, and a couple of bigger fish kept circling in within range. I fished with the old orange quill and it moved about three times for various small carp before it turned slowly and slid away across the surface. I struck. It wasn't one of the small ones. The centre-pin screamed. That fish really got moving, straight out for about twenty yards. The Hardy was buckled into its battle curve as I felt the fish strike some submerged obstacle. It then headed right and I held it hard. I felt the line rubbing. I didn't like it. There was a swirl and it was over. The hook-hold had gone - though when I reeled it in I found the point turned over as if it had come up against some very hard surface. I sang a lament up to the flying grey clouds, and went back to my pitch for a fresh hook. But I didn't get another touch. *[Am I getting the feeling that fate, or Redmire, or Izaak has decreed that I'm not destined to land anything over 20 lb this year?]*

As the sun went down into a bank of blue-black cloud, so the wind suddenly began to die. The ripples smoothed and faded and the trees stood still and silent.

I sat by my stove, cooking a delicious meal of cod in wine sauce, and looking out at the gently dying day.

Wednesday, 5th October

Woke early to listen to Elgar's 'Egdon Heath' on the radio I brought this time. The music matched perfectly the grey and blue sky, the white half-moon and a rainbow.

I re-cast all rods and by 9.30 there were bubbles rising just about everywhere. I was sure a fish would take one of the baits and at about 10.0, just after a herd of cattle had gone past me, up the track behind the bushes, I heard the quick hiss. But I was too slow to realise what was happening. The big fold of foil had risen and then slid back down. I'd thought it had stopped, but the line was still tightening. I picked up the rod, leant forward and waited for the line to tighten again. But it never moved. That was all that the morning brought.

I went down to the village at lunch-time to get some more cheese, as one of the farm dogs had stolen all I had. When I got back, I took the Hardy round to the far bank, to the platform again. But I couldn't see anything. There were one or two big fish off the island, but nothing like yesterday. I wandered back and had an urge to fish by the withy roots, 'just for five minutes'.

I cast a little further than usual, though still not above twenty feet from the trailing branches.

The wind was up again, but the trees sheltered the water below them and there was only a slight drift and ripple on the surface. The float lay flat for five minutes, then it changed direction. Was a carp down there? Two leaves drifted past the orange quill. The float turned again after another few minutes, but this time there was no doubt, it was sliding very gently away. I struck and the reel screamed, but the bloody line was caught round the reel rest - though that wasn't fatal. I didn't like it and fumbled to unhitch it. The carp had shot for a few yards to the left. As I freed the line he turned and bolted straight out. The line went slack. Tragic loss is the worst sensation. I punched the tree trunk next to me. I punched the ground. That fish had left a trail of mud across the shallows a yard wide. I ripped the size 8 from the line and vowed never to use them again (this week!). *[Somewhere in the world there must be a hook pattern that will conform to my non-conformist techniques.]*

When I'd got over the feeling of murderous violence, I tied on a 6 and went back to the roots for another go. Twice the quill slid across the surface, one even going under; but both times were too fast and hesitant. I hooked no more fish. As the sun began to near the horizon, so the wind died.

Back in the Fence, having my tea, I noticed a few bubbles showing about thirty yards out. Within half an hour the whole area of water in front of me was a frothing mass. I cast all rods, and within minutes of casting the Avon the silver paper hissed on it for a brief second. That was all the bubbles could produce. After half an hour more, they disappeared with the fading day.

Thursday, 6th October

The wind was blowing from the east when I looked out of my bivouac in the morning. A fish rolled again by the Stile. That decided it. I stayed put for an hour or two, hoping some bubbler would come my way; then I moved the whole lot round in two trips - one for the rods and net (easy) and one for the brolly, brolly-camp, bedding, food, stove, pressure-cooker, tackle box, water etc. That new bag I got in Ross was a good buy (I only tottered once - coming over the dam stile).

Within an hour I was repositioned in the Stile Pitch, the rods out, a cup of tea in my hands.

A light rain began to strengthen. By 3 p.m. it was coming down quite hard. I'd had one pull, within seconds of casting one of the rods - but I think it was a line-catch. Somehow, I wasn't confident with the yellow gramms. I kept thinking about the big fish I saw picking up cockles last June. I thought a damp, moist autumn, when the carp are beginning to look for something juicy before the cold weather comes in, would be an even better cockle-popping time. For a while, I thought about it. Then I was doing something about it; driving through the rain to Ross. Typically, I couldn't find any cockles; but there were frozen prawns in one shop and that was a good, if expensive second best. I was back in my pitch by 5.30, baiting up two rods as soon as the prawns had defrosted.

At 7.0, I went to a telephone box in the village and had a jolly chat to Clare. Then I phoned Bob Jones, who insisted I try peas at the earliest convenience. One day, when the big boys are up under the trees in the shallows, I'll see whether they like 'em or not (as Rod says they hate 'em).

Made a superb meal when I got back. The only good thing the Tories ever did was sell me that pressure-cooker! Slept soundly.

Friday, 7th October

Woke at about 8.40. I re-baited the prawn rods and then made a cup of tea. I was halfway through it when the silver paper on a prawn rod, rose up and the line began to peel slowly from the Ambidex. I rolled forward, jettisoning my tea-cup on the way, picked up the rod, hesitated, then struck. A solid resistance began to head to the right. The rod curved over - at least (I hoped) I could break the week's blank - if only the hook would hold. The line was new 9.4 Platil S. No worries there. The fish ran into weed and stuck there for a second or two while I slowly eased him out. Then he swung straight in and I knew he was no big 'un. In went the net and I hoisted a tough little common on to the bank. The hook was well down, an uncomfortable position for the fish; but a good sign, as it shows how confident he was with this new bait.

The sun came out. I felt better. At least I wasn't going to blank.

Down in the Willow Pitch was a 'permanent' bubbler. I went to get my rod. I cast a prawn, but the bait flew off. A mole surfaced next to me and a worm slithered out of his hole. I put the worm on the hook, thinking I must not look a gift mole in the mouth, and cast towards the bubbler.

After five minutes, the silver paper slid across the board of wood on the bank. The line jerked out and I struck, rather too hastily I feel. The mole tunnelled away, disgusted. I wasn't rattled by the miss. As I sneaked back to my pitch, I was feeling confident there would be another chance. I even said to myself, "You're going to get one, ain't you!"

I climbed the Island Tree and spotted one or two fish beginning to move up the shallows. A breeze had sprung up, more to the south than yesterday, but the sun was warming the water.

After an hour I set up a rod from the platform. But as things looked quiet, I brought up another, C.S. III, which can cast a bait with ease for a long way, owing to the 7.4 Platil on the 300. I cast out a yard short of the trailing branches of the opposite willows, and after only a few minutes I had a short twitch on the silver paper. It came again. Then the rod next to it also had a more positive pull. I waited as it pulled again, then I struck quickly but missed. Eels? I re-cast both rods and sat back to listen to a chamber concert on the radio. (Just as well none of the other syndicate members were here!) As the quiet strains of a Beethoven sonata drifted across the shallows, I climbed the climbing tree. The sun was bright and I could make out four quite good fish over by the withy roots. They turned and headed towards the '35' pitch. Not far from there was my furthest bait. I looked down and could easily see the two silver papers on the platform. Neither moved.

Ravel replaced Beethoven and I stayed up the tree, watching for any large dark shapes to appear. I heard a quick rustle and looked back to the platform. The silver paper on C.S. III had jammed in the butt ring. It was quivering!

I seemed to get in a great knot as I slid frantically out of the willow. Then round the overgrown path, on to the platform. The line was still streaming out, the little fold of foil hissing in stutters. I picked up the rod, flicked in the pick-up and didn't strike but just wound down until I couldn't wind anymore. The long line stretched out and to the right. A slow surge began to make the 'C' clutch squeal. I looked across the water and could just make out a boil in the surface right over by Greenbanks. There was another, slow powerful surge. Two coots under Bowskill's Tree suddenly fluttered round in a circle, looking down below them. The line must have tickled their feet. They were seventy-five yards away!

I even pulled an extra few yards of line from the reel to ease the strain of a suddenly more powerful surge. On the light tackle, I didn't want too much pressure early on, rather let the fish tire by doing all the pulling himself. I was remembering, with a qualm, the submerged branches I'd seen near Bowskill's Tree, when the fish began to ease off and turn towards the islands. I increased pressure and after a while he swung diagonally across the shallows, heading very powerfully towards the trailing branches of the willow in the '35'. The clutch rang. I brought the rod point over and down, wincing as I braced myself for the first 'ping' of the line on a snag. But there was no 'ping'. He'd got past the branches but was now heading for even more dangerous terrain, the sunken willow and the jungle of shoots up by the top end of the shallows. "If he gets in there," I told myself, "you're done!"

I gave the line as much as it would take. The fish swirled, rolled and hung for a moment. I wound down, but he made another forceful bid. I couldn't give him an inch; he was that close. I held on and the rod went right over and made a brittle 'tinging' sound. I applied sidestrain from the left and it worked. He swung round, pulled, then gave it up and headed back down the lake, but keeping over to the far side. I piled on more pressure as he approached the '35' branches, but he was soon well past them, moving quickly. When he came opposite, I managed to steer him round and began pumping with long, steady pulls. He was coming now. At least I would get a glimpse of him, even if the hook did pull. He swung past me and nearly made a dive for the bush on my left. But I held him off and brought him back. He didn't look nearly as big as I thought he'd be. A small carp of about 5 lb was following him and he was not much more than three times the junior's size. A solid-looking common though, well worth every moment of the waiting, but not the expected 20. I got the net ready and rolled him towards it, lifting as soon as he was over the draw-string. He thrashed, pushing to the right. But I'd got him now. A great, fat, sleek, golden common. A beautiful fish, as much as I wanted - or needed - today. A fish that had contested every inch but who, in the end, was safely hammocked in the landing net. I felt elated at having won against the odds; not just the odds of the moment, but the odds that seem to have been stacking up against me all season. And am I developing a persecution complex? And am I becoming neurotic? Maybe I am, but this classic carp has saved me - at least for the time being.

I could have spent the rest of the bright evening in the pub but I went into the village instead, just to see if they had any prawns. They had! And they even split a packet up for me so I only had to buy as much of this expensive bait as I needed. But how do you weigh the expense against the value - the value of its deadliness as a bait. I would have paid twice what I did and still felt I'd got a bargain. Yet when I got back it was as if a door had closed over Redmire. I had had my fish; now everything was withdrawing and there was an eerie stillness about the place, that intensified as it grew dark. Perhaps something had disturbed the Redmire ghost, but not even my fresh sweet prawns could disturb any more carp.

Wednesday, 26th October - Redmire

That's the first time there's been no other fishing days to break up the fortnightly interval - too much work. In fact it was lucky I got here at all. It's the latest I've ever fished at Redmire, though the season has yet to turn cold and the weather, for the first part of the week anyway, has been like summer.

I arrived with only enough light left to set up in the willow and get one rod out. Then I made tea and settled down to listen to Britten's violin concerto on the new radio. The music matched perfectly the scene of the dark trees and the full moon showing fitfully through the rushing cloud. Ten minutes after it was over, the silver paper on the Avon and centre-pin hissed. As I was scrabbling with the canvas flap, the reel screeched. I got my hands to the rod but it had stopped.

I was using prawns and, heartened by the quick response, I set up two more rods and caught two eels.

Thursday, 27th October

A couple of slow runs disturbed my dreams, but I left them, convinced it was eels again. I climbed the Island Tree after breakfast and saw only one, slow-moving carp. A big common. There was nothing in the shallows.

The day soon ended, biteless, and as it got dark the cloud that had been with me almost all day, cleared for the moon. A big fish rolled, a long way up the lake and I watched and waited for the slow waves to come down to the deep end, breaking up the moon's still reflection.

Friday, 28th October

Nothing. I climbed the tree, and there were a couple of fish out in the centre. But a cool breeze was blowing. Down in Langarren there'd been a heavy frost. The breeze was coming from that cold valley and chilled the water. The lines never moved.

By mid afternoon, I decided to move up to Inghams and, quickly setting up camp between brief showers of rain, I was glad of my change of scene. Inghams is a neglected little spot and it seemed I was settling down in green, virgin territory. But not a touch did I have.

The moon was clear again after dark and the night cold. Just after midnight a tremendous flock of rooks passed noisily over the pool, plainly visible against the luminous sky. Had they a premonition of some planetary disaster?

Saturday, 29th October

As I slept, clouds covered the sky and the temperature rose so that I woke sweating and had to remove a couple of layers before I was comfortable again.

I woke late. The rods were still asleep. The prawns didn't seem to be working. I made breakfast after re-casting all rods and while I sipped my tea, a big carp rolled just a few yards from the overhanging branches of the alder. At least I'd seen a Redmire carp in his autumn colours.

I went into Ross before midday and bought a pound of frozen cockles. The prawns didn't smell appetizing and, anyway, cockles were what I wanted in the first place - and they're twice as cheap. I had a chat with Dave Bufton on my way back and we spoke about badgers, but I really couldn't wait and was glad when he went off to his lunch so that I could cast out my new bait (as it turned out I had to wait a bit for the things to thaw).

The cockles cast, I decided to have a quick look from the Island Tree as the sun had come out suddenly and the breeze was milder. But I waited five minutes before I saw anything: a common of perhaps 18 lb. Two more carp appeared, heading up to the shallows. But then, as the breeze began to stiffen, they turned. There was a vague dark carp-shaped form in the middle of a lighter area of mud that at first glance I thought was a very big carp, but then realised was simply too big. However, when I glanced back at it, the dark mass slowly redefined itself, rising like an airship out of the lighter patch - it *was* a carp, a real monster. He settled down again and, as I watched, a pale cloud of mud billowed up all round him; he seemed to be fanning the bottom with his fins . . .

[Break here for a dive out into the moonlight to strike at run. Slow (deceptive?) pull, but he didn't get much line, even though it was the 7.4 Platil. The rod kept hard over as I worked it slowly in (fumbling with this lot and putting shoes on at the same time). I was just expecting it to break surface when there came that sensation, as if a chasm has opened and either you or the fish has dropped down into it. I was standing on the end of the platform, my heart pounding in my ears.]

Now, where was I? Ah yes . . . the pale area I'd been mystified by - a billowing cloud of mud with the huge shape lying in the middle. He was heartachingly huge, too. He inched forward into clearer water and I could see that he was even more than just huge - he was colossal. He was a leather, a very dark-looking leather; and, furthermore, he was almost directly in line with my left-hand bait - mooching slowly down the pool towards it.

I hurried back to my pitch and prepared for a possible drama. The line went out jerkily on the right-hand rod. I struck, and in came a horrible little eel. I got the hook back, though. I was just about to re-cast when the line went smoothly out on the left-hand rod, the Hardy. Before the silver paper had hit the ring, I picked up the rod in my left hand and struck.

What a sensation! I couldn't believe it to begin with and thought it was an eel with his tail round a sunken branch. But then came an incredibly powerful surge, the rod went over almost flat and the clutch snarled. I eased off, a tactic I regret now. The carp went steadily out like a slow tugboat. He sounded twenty-five yards off the Fence. I wound down, gained a foot and lost a yard. A great patch of bubbles broke surface seventy yards away, and then a MASSIVE fin appeared, cutting from left to right. "The Hardy!" I said, "You've done it again!" I kicked the other rod in and threw the net in after it. The fish 'gave' and I had a horrible feeling the hook had gone; but he was still there. Now was the time to really get bending. Though the line was only 8 I was only applying about ³/₄ pressure and was holding the fish 'comfortably' on a half curved rod.

My adversary moved on slowly right until he was opposite me, right over the far side. I hadn't felt any drag of weed and was beginning to think this was merely going to be a lengthy but trouble-free battle. The carp was still pulling, then hanging, and I pumped on a clutch set far too light. He went away again. The rod went down, the clutch sang. He stopped, turned, began to dive into Pitchford's Pit, and then the whole landscape jerked back from me and I wound frantically, but it kept falling further and further away.

This is perhaps the worst loss I've ever had. Will ever have. Right at the end of the season, after a series of unlucky mishaps - all with big fish. I felt drained and bitter. I cursed with everything and ripped a dead elm tree right out of the ground and hurled it over the hedge.

Having once experienced the sensation of a carp on the line of almost 44 lb, I can say with absolute certainty that I'd just lost something much bigger.

After I'd got over the first shock, I re-cast the rods, and jotted down a report in the catch-book. As I was doing that, a silver paper indicator slid loudly across the old wooden platform. I dropped everything but my pen (which I held in my teeth), rolled forward and then struck, long and far back. There was a solid connection with . . . well at least it wasn't an eel. It kept the rod bent double, but I wasn't going to let this one get away and he wasn't big enough to pull more than a few inches off the clutch. In he came, slowly, splashing on the top. I got him over the net but he dived out and I swung him back and held him this time.

Well, at least I haven't blanked. A beautiful, fat, gold common lay on the grass. I wish he'd had a pound for every scale on his lateral line (38). As it was he was just under 7.

It began to darken. There were no more steady runs, just hesitant jerks, for jerk eels. One was a big one, but it got me in a terrible, slimy mess and I had to completely re-tackle both rods . . . The moon rose above the ash tree on Greenbanks. I made my supper, wrote this, then lost that previously mentioned fish - a fish, I pray was only as small as I think.

The eels kept me disturbed until midnight, when I reeled in. At least I slept soundly.

Sunday, 30th October

When I woke up I relished the thought of going back to sleep. For a while I lay there. Then I forced myself up, re-baited and re-cast left and right. Then I made tea and, while it was brewing, served myself some peaches and ate them with muesli and milk. Thus fortified, I turned off Schubert's 4th and listened to the far more exquisite sounds of the birds and their autumn songs. I had my tea and began to jot some notes in my other journal.

I wrote, sitting in my sleeping-bag, the breeze strengthening to a wind and then, for a few minutes, dying back to a breeze.

There was a hiss and my papers went everywhere as I rolled forward and grabbed the Hardy. In my awkward, impossible position, I made a solid strike and was overjoyed at the response. No eel, but then I knew it wasn't an eel. The clutch rang out, there was a (small) splash and the little rod bowed down to a fast and powerful carp. As it ran I somehow managed to get my shoes on and step on to the end of the platform. The carp kept going, running parallel with the bank so that I had to keep the rod tip low to avoid the line catching against the alder on my left. Eventually, after about a thirty yard dash, he slowed down and I began to gain a few yards. I wasn't going to make the same mistake as yesterday. Though I knew I may lose this fish and had prepared myself for that, I wasn't going to lose it through being too namby. The rod was rigidly hooped and the line sang in the wind. Gradually, I worked him back until I saw a big swirl that made a flat spot in the ripples fifteen yards out. He turned and went down, and I let him have a few yards before tightening up again and rolling him round. I'd seen the scaled flank. He was a good fish. I didn't want to lose him now I'd seen him clearly.

I made sure the other rod had its tip well down in the water, then I gave the tackle as much as it would take and a dark shape began to show under the grey ripples, coming in towards me. But he turned and surged strongly to the right. Kiting in there, he would have meshed me among a forest of brambles. For a long half minute, I was worried, but I managed to ease him back, back into the clear water in front of me. He rolled, and I felt the awful 'twang' of line as it rubbed against his dorsal and flank. He turned again and I kept the pressure on him as I got the net ready with my left hand. I drew him half over the cord, but then he bolted out, running just a few yards before I stopped him and swung him back (I slipped on the platform and got a wet right foot). Those last few seconds were smooth and quick, yet agonising. I couldn't believe the hook would pull at such a moment, yet I guessed it might. Over the mesh came his head, then his bronze bulk; he was lying half on his side and it was easier that second time. I lifted the net and he was deep in the mesh, splashing but safe. I dragged him in through the greenery alongside the platform and then bent down to look at him. He was a beautiful fish. Solid, rotund, immaculate condition and the gold turning to deep orange under the wrist of the tail. He really was solid and I knew I mustn't guess the weight as I'd probably be wrong. But I was well satisfied when the needle on the balance touched 16½ lb. I know I'm not destined to take a 20 this year, but with moments like these, I don't mind. He was 26 ½ inches from nose to fork of tail (29 inches nose to tail). I photographed him after waiting an hour to see if I could make it a group portrait. I let him go from the Ruins and he looked strong and sullen as he pushed out towards the deeps.

The wind grew to a gale. The leaves flew in showers. The lines didn't move for a carp again and by 12.30 there was no one fishing at Inghams. There was no one fishing at Redmire at all and I drove home for tea, with the wind behind me.

Tuesday, 16th November

Last week had been perfect. The weather soft, the breezes strong but mild. I had little work to do, yet I couldn't manage to break from my few engagements and go again to Redmire. With no rota, I could go when I pleased. Tom even said I could take Rod with me.

Yesterday, I made a brief check of the rods. Even got the pressure-cooker out, ready for loading. But there had been a whole winter's weather since this time last week. Storms, flooding - even hurricanes. This morning, I stood on the front lawn, watching my breath come out in clouds. Even then I was undecided. Would it be warmer further west? Should I begin loading the van? It was hopeless. It was the low forties. By the evening, as Clare and I walked up the long slope from Chussex, the grass was brittle with frost, grey in the soft moonlight.

So I'm glad I didn't go - to shiver under canvas and cast into lifeless water. Perhaps there will be another warm spell to get the carp moving. Perhaps . . .

14th March, 1978 - Redmire

. . . there was. The second week in March was the warmest I can remember. But I couldn't make it to Redmire then. There was too
much bloody work, too much bloody jazzing around generally. Luckily Rick had decided Friday would be a good day to go chub fishing
on the Mole. But what a day! The sun was like summer. There were
even dace rising for flies. I could imagine what Redmire was like. I
reckoned the carp would have been basking. Anyway, we had a good
day on the river. Rick had the best day's fishing he'd ever had, he
said. He had nine chub! I had six and a lovely roach that came from
under the Forest Swim just as it was getting dark. It was the best
Mole roach I've caught. The weekend was warm, but busy and even
Monday took too long, though I'd planned to at least get to Redmire
by nightfall. I managed to load the van in the morning, but on my
way back from London in the afternoon, two problems set me back.
One: the weather took a nasty turn. Two: I couldn't get any cockles.

The wind howled, the rain poured. Damn it! I'd leave at dawn
and sleep in a dry bed.

Come the dawn, the dawn to the last day of the season, the wind
roared outside my window and the rain clawed on the glass. The
birds were beginning to wake, but I couldn't. It sounded mean out
there. I just curled up like a craven mouse and went back to sleep.
It was Dad who eventually roused me - at 7 a.m.

"Come on you sod," I told myself, "Redmire awaits!"

By 8.0 I was on my way. The traffic was manic to begin with, but
I got through it and, apart from losing a wiper, made Ross in good
time, though I had a fierce wind to fight against and that slowed me.

I was in Ross at 11.40 and there, in the deep-freeze at the
Centre was a box of cockles. I bought some lead from the tackle

shop, where the old lady remembered Dick Walker, the Taylor Brothers and Maurice Ingham, and was coming down the drive to Redmire by 2.10.

It was a beautiful day to be back and though the pool had been ravaged by the winter winds, with dead trees lying in the water, though the oaks were bare and the wind whistled through the black poplars, it all looked as lovely as I imagined it would.

By 1.0 I had set up at Inghams and was, once again, sitting in my bivouac, a mug of hot tea in my hands and the rods lying on the landing stage. The wind flapped at the canvas, the clouds glided over, the water rippled and showers of rain ringed it. A rainbow showed through the trees. What more could a man ask?

The silver paper hissed. I picked up the wrong rod in my out-of-practice panic. The line was still moving. I struck on the right rod. And missed!

I'd been thinking, perhaps the carp have yet to recover from the freeze-up of last month, when Redmire must have been covered in thick ice and the fields deep in snow. But there . . . there was something. Probably an eel, though. I re-cast.

At about 3.0, I went for a look up in the shallows. The water was wind-blown and I couldn't see. I climbed the tree and got cold as I waited for a sign below me.

It was good to get back to the bivouac, out of the wind. It wasn't really a cold wind, not for March, but it was strong. At about 3.30 I had confirmation that the Redmire carp were not asleep. A streaming run on the Hardy that I hit fair and square. It was certainly no eel. The clutch on my new Ambidex sounded like a bumble-bee trapped in the spinning works, and the fish made a tremendous run from far left to far right. It just kept on going for the dam and, though I leaned out on the end of the platform, the line was coming dangerously near the overhanging branches of the alder on my right.

There is a dead elm lying in deep water at the corner of the dam. I realise now that as the carp ran on, it was that tree he was trying to get to. The rod was pulled down again and the clutch buzzed. If I had remembered the elm tree then I bet I would have fallen over! As it was, the fish turned without quite getting far enough and I began drawing it back, kicking the other rod in the water and dragging the net over to me, all in wild, awkward movements. I felt a 'twang' on the line. But it was all right. He was swimming straight towards me now, coming in almost too quickly. He sounded. The rod went hard over and I couldn't shift him. I couldn't tell how far away he was, though the angle of the line was now in the 'safe' position, heading straight out. I increased pressure and 'blip'! The lead flipped up only forty feet away; he'd been as near as that, and I'd lost him. The hook had slipped. Again. [*If I could claim compensation from Lion d'Or for every big carp I've lost on their hooks I'd be the richest man in the world.*]

I reckon I took it quite calmly - for about five minutes. Then I buried my head in a mole-hill and swore so loudly it must have echoed in the bowels of the earth. Did it make it any better? Yes!

The Hardy again. It seems a miracle (or a disaster) to have hooked and lost so many good fish on that rod. It was so nearly another one in the bag - so nearly. 20 plus? 30 plus? Well, nothing I've landed these last few seasons felt remotely like it. That initial charge down the pool was simply fantastic.

I re-cast, had a slow run on C.S. III and hooked a 2 lb eel. Now it's 5.30. Only another hour of daylight. Only six-and-a-half hours left of the season. But it's been a great season, however anguished I was at times. And it may yet finish with a further touch of magic. Right now, I think I'll have a cup of tea . . .

The wind seemed to strengthen as it got dark. When a big gust came over, it made the cables at the edge of the barley-field roar like a crowd. In between gusts, I listened for the sound of silver paper.

The crescent moon appeared in gaps in the reeling clouds and the stars were brilliant. The high clouds seemed to go over too slowly when I imagined the strength of the wind up there.

I had a fast run on C.S. III that made me very hopeful. I was still hopeful when I struck and felt a deep throb. But soon the throb changed to a wiggle and up came a bloody eel. I got my feet wet diving for another run, an hour later. Again it was an eel.

I had my hot dinner and even my feet warmed up!

Then, with a cup of tea, I blew out the candle and stuck my head outside, watching the last minutes of the season tick away. It had been, as I said, a great season - it could have been greater if only I'd landed more of the bigger carp I'd hooked. But those losses made my few successes so much sweeter and it gave my carp fishing a new edge. I've never been so keen as I am now. I've never enjoyed my fishing so much.

The silver paper shot up to the ring on the Hardy. There it stopped. I crouched behind it, ready for the instant strike . . .

Season 19

June 1978 - March 1979

Bliss!
Another
wet
teatime

16th June - Lodge Pond, Farnham

The moon was bright in the cold, misty air as we four (Nick, Jasper and Anglepen) made our casts. It was too cold though, and the heavy fall of rain earlier in the evening had ensured the night would stay cold. But the moisture was producing some typically lovely June smells and, owing to the mini-drought of the past weeks, I had been missing those early summer fragrances.

The carp were not much in evidence. Jasper landed a small mirror (5 lb) after only half an hour and I woke up from a shallow sleep to hear Nick land an 8 pounder. Come the mist filled dawn, I thought I was bound to open the season with a good carp, but it wasn't until after midday that a fish came to the baits. Unfortunately I wasn't at my rods at the time and Jasper struck at a long run and broke the line, which was lighter than he thought.

We went for a splendid pub lunch then, marvelling at the improved weather, remarking at the huge white clouds that had floated over all morning, disparaging the behaviour of all the carp anglers we'd seen (because of their electronic irritators) and delighting in the fact that we were the only ones to have contacted any fish.

Back at the pond, I couldn't shake off my tiredness and just lay in the sun, half asleep. Maybe the carp felt the same as me; maybe I was affecting them; maybe they were affecting me.

Nick landed a nice looking 'wild' common of about 7 lb, giving him a satisfactory brace next to my astoundingly thorough blank. I'll have to catch up with him on some less noted water, for I'm sure that's why sport was so slow. Too many hundredweights of bait had gone in over the preceding weeks and the carp were almost too full to move. I bet they're sick of particles. Oh, for a cockle, I thought.

Tuesday, 20th June - Johnson's Lake, Kent

Drove down to Kent to see Rod at Johnson's Lakes. There he was, listening to a sermon from Fred Wilton. I showed him my new cane rods but nothing impressed him like the old Hardy.

"Give us a run with it," he said, so I hooked the line to the back of the van and drove off. He pumped it back after a hundred yard run!

It was all talk and no fishing. We sat outside the Bricklayer's Arms, watching the sun touch the North Downs, drinking and discussing the world. Despite his continuing enthusiasm for all things carpish, Rod was unusually critical about carp anglers themselves. "Where are the real carp fishers nowadays?" he asked. "What happened to them all? Are there any left?"

It was dark by the time I set up, and dawn by the time I thought I might get a fish. But I didn't. Rod got a 6 lb 5 oz tench. I netted it. The biggest tench I've ever seen. No one caught a carp.

Tuesday, 27th June - Redmire Pool

After a hard day, it wasn't until midnight that I'd got everything ready. It was, in fact, the 27th, Tuesday, when I kissed Clare good-bye and drove off into the night. By Abingdon a blue light was already touching the north-eastern sky and it was only 2.30 a.m. There was a mist in the Windrush Valley. At 4.15 I was coasting down the hill to the pool, the birds singing in the cold, grey dawn.

I've never seen, I don't think, the weed so thick. There were plenty of holes fishable, but it was as good as the old days, even lush and green up in the shallows where I sat for an hour with the Hardy and a quill. Nothing moved. There were bubbles, but it was only disturbed mud. Nothing leapt or even disturbed the surface. It was too cold and I was glad that John Carver had woken up and, seeing me creeping around, offered me a welcome cup of tea. I sat with him in his pitch and he told me I hadn't been missing anything. Hardly a fish had stirred since his arrival on Sunday.

By 10.0 I had set up in the Fence; the best bet on the pool, I guessed, as the weed converged there but didn't mass in front of it. I cast out two cockle rods and was just going to sleep when I heard a brief hiss. A bloody eel! I cast again and slept till 5 p.m.

I went round for more tea and some supper with John. After the meal I went to see how the new-bug was doing. Barry Mills starts his Redmire fishing this week and for him, he said, this week will always be memorable, win or lose. I had a long talk with him and ended up thinking how lucky I was to have two such good blokes on this rota when the chances were I'd be fishing with morons! Barry especially is not just interesting on angling topics, he's got a wonderful attitude towards life.

But the good conversation made me miss what might have been a carp. I'd been keeping an eye on my distant foil indicator and suddenly noticed that it was in the butt ring. Instantly I raced over to it. I wound up, but all was solid in the weed. When I slacked off, the loose line drew tight, yet I couldn't get the fish on top, or move it at all once I'd tightened up again. Maybe it was just another eel. As it was, the line suddenly began to come free and I reeled in to find the hook gone but the link and stop all right. The 8 lb Sylcast was too light for these conditions. Barry gave me some 11 lb Platil which I'm now fishing with - the bait waiting for a monster - back under the tree.

Wednesday, 28th June

Woke to find the rain pattering down on the canvas and a strong breeze blowing. Fell asleep again for a few more hours and woke to find the sun warm in a blue sky. Got up, eventually, and had a look round. No carp were moving in the shallows, no carp were moving anywhere. But I reckoned the warm sun, after so many cold days, would gradually get them going again. We went into Ross for provisions and returned at 2.30 to find that I was right - the carp were moving. From the tree in the shallows I spotted one or two cruisers moving up to the top island. I took my rod there and for an hour I fished. Two or three big carp came close to the baits, but none came near enough. There was a lot of activity by my 'tussock', so I went round there and knew, as I did so, I would get a fish. I got my little orange quill, put on some corn and flicked the tackle out to the edge of the weeds (this was after I'd tried cockles and had a 20 common nose down to it right under the rod tip, then swim off). Bubbles were rising and within a few minutes the float moved once, then turned and slid to the left. I struck and a bow wave surged out. I lost only a few yards and as the fish rolled I could see he was only an infant compared to the monsters all round me. After a little slog I slid him up on to the muddy margin. A perfect, deep gold common of $7\frac{3}{4}$ lb.

I had another chance later on, but struck too soon. The fish were still moving well and I should have persevered with a cockle instead of going for another long chat, over a cup of tea, with John and Barry.

As it grew dark the cool wind dropped and the lake was silent and warm and sweet smelling.

Thursday, 29th June

The continuous rain of the morning cooled the pool and slowed the fish down. A grey breeze blew all afternoon and there were not nearly the same numbers of carp in the shallows as yesterday. Not until 11 p.m. with my quill silhouetted against faint streaks of light still in the sky, did a fish show any interest in my baits. I had dropped a bean under the willow branch and a carp stirred the float and humped at the surface. But it was too dark to see properly and I didn't strike. The bait was still there when I reeled in, anyway.

Great banks of cloud floated like whales against the afterglow in the west. There had been a rich, glowing sunset, bursting out under the dense layers; now the sky was dark and serene, yet the 'whales' were beginning to mass even as I retired under canvas. Now, after midnight, the wind has returned and my breath is showing in the candlelight.

Friday, 30th June

Woke late to a breeze and warm sunshine. Had a cup of tea and, after a while, went for a stroll under the willows by the shallows. No carp were moving.

Had a talk about property with John and Barry. Barry was pleased with his first Redmire carp - a 4-5 pounder with scattered mirror-common scaling. Just like a jewel from the water, he said.

I climbed the Island Tree and saw a lot of big carp lying in the weed, their grey-blue backs occasionally humping on the surface.

But they were just dozing in the sun, not a single fish moved. So I went and had some dinner - herring in sauce, new potatoes, green pepper and courgettes (this was just after a visit to Ross for more cockles).

As evening drew on, the ripples in the barley-field opposite and the ripples on the surface, began to die down. I went to the willows again, with the Hardy this time, but nothing had moved up, yet. So I went on, leaving the rod on a forked stick and walked into the field, and passed the barns to the top of the valley side where I looked out at the white sun behind milky cloud. Orcop Hill and the Black Mountains beyond. The breeze was still moving up there, only a breath though. Behind me the pool, lying between the lines of trees, cupped in the valley's palm. I thought of all the men who had spent their days crouched there - of all the hopes and intense emotions experienced there and the moments of triumph and bitter disappointment. All in the unhurried, somehow mysterious pursuit of a big carp. And whether I was successful or not, I was part of a continuing tradition, like all those that had gone before and like myself in previous years, I was allowing the pool and its surroundings to draw me into its slow, unpredictable rhythm, I was allowing myself to be immersed in a different world. I was more watchful, more subdued, more calm, except for those moments of close concentration and nervous anticipation and, sometimes, relief and fulfilment when a big carp finally lay beaten on the bankside grass. If I had the choice, I thought, as I came back down the barley-field, I'd stay here all summer, only going home at weekends to see Clare, and not bother with work. Is that a strange choice? Not really. To want to live in tranquillity and natural beauty is not a strange desire. And the giant carp? Maybe that's not so strange either.

Carp were moving in the shallows when I got back. I brought up two rods, a cushion, my fur-coat and tea-making gear, as I planned to sit out the night under the willows and I knew it wasn't going to be warm.

One rod went out on cockle, one on corn (the Hardy). Almost immediately a big carp moved over the cockle. But the line was still. Then I had a slow run, but missed. Re-casting to the same place, though, and beyond an overhanging willow branch, I soon had another good run and struck into what I thought was a small carp but which turned out to be a bloody great eel. The biggest I've ever caught - over 4 lb, with a mouth like a pike's. Luckily, I caught no more like him.

Saturday, 1st July

Half-past midnight. I made a cup of tea, shielding the blue glow of the flame from the water with my body. Twenty minutes later, as I was leaning back against the willow trunk, half dreaming, a sharp hiss brought me to my senses. Why I wondered which rod it was on I don't know. Only carp runs came to the Hardy (it *was* a carp run). I struck and a fish bolted out to my right, through the branch and on into the weed-bed beyond. I must have been more sleepy than I thought, for it was a few minutes before I really came out of my daze and began to think clearly. He was pulling well. The clutch was still going in fits and starts. I'd thought it was only small, but as the line came clear of some of the branches and I got a direct pull on it in the weeds, I knew it was a fair fish. I got it back to the branch but I stuck there. I let it go, drew it in, and it got stuck again. I pondered awhile. It seemed well hooked, so I went in for it, expecting to sink into the ooze, but finding the bottom much firmer than I thought. I got to the carp, sorted it out and had to drop the rod in the water to grab the fish, unhook it and, somehow, carry it above. Then I went back for the poor muddied Hardy and pulled in all the weed and branch still on the line.

When I'd sorted it out I had a look at the carp properly. It was a big, sleek, strong common, superbly proportioned, glimmering like some kind of live metal in the dark. I slipped him into a sack, proposing to find out his number on the scales in the morning.

I went round the shallows to tell Barry about my little saga. He too was sitting up all night and I said I'd watch his rods while he nipped off to get a bottle of drink from his pitch in Inghams. While he was gone, one of his luminous floats slowly dissolved into the darkness and I watched his supplementary silver paper. It didn't move. Barry returned and struck; as he was doing so, the float began to reappear! I should've struck earlier - but I didn't want to risk messing his swim up with just a pricked fish. He had another bite a few minutes later, just as I was sitting under my willow having another cup of tea. He missed again.

Big carp were moving round me. One kept returning to the same spot, just along the margins from me, burrowing his head into the mud. It sounded like someone screwing a post into the bottom - the hiss of bubbles was as loud as that. But already it was getting light again. It seemed only an hour since dark, yet now a pale blue showed in the north-east and in a while a skylark began to sing in the fading gloom. Above me, the willow leaves began to grow harder and clearer out of the sky. A cock crowed. Then I looked to the horizon again and a big crescent moon had come up behind the milky cloud. It glowed pale yellow in the pale blue. The carp gradually dispersed and by the time it was light enough to see detail, they were all gone from the shallows.

Barry went back to his pitch for a sleep. There was a faint rushing sound that I thought, for a second, was water cascading over the dam! Then I came to my senses and realised it was the black poplars catching a high breeze. All the other trees, though, were dead still. The breeze was passing high over the valley and not coming down to it. I checked my carp and discovered it had burst through the top of the sack and escaped. Pity, as it would've made a splendid portrait. Also, I'd wanted to show it to Barry. An hour later I went back to the Fence, and within moments the distant birdcalls and splashing of moorhens were getting fainter and fainter . . .

Woke at 11 a.m. to find that both John and Barry had decided to leave a day early. So I was left with the pool to myself. But I might as well have gone too, as far as the fishing was concerned. There were absolutely no chances and not a single fish moved all day. Watching the clouds drift by and seeing the sky darken, I didn't really care about the fish though, I was just glad I was here.

Sunday, 2nd July

Woke at 6.0, though I thought it was around 11.0! Again, no carp were moving, though I cast out hopefully, putting my baits just where I wanted them, yet not really putting them there with any faith. I didn't want to admit that I wasn't going to catch anything on this last morning, yet I knew, somehow, I wouldn't.

For six hours I waited; not a fish rolled or bubbled in all that time and when I climbed the look-out trees not one carp appeared below me. The wind blew, the lake looked almost stunned from all the bad weather and it seemed to me that it was frowning. I reeled in my baits, made a last cup of tea and drove slowly away up the field and along the track, across the cattle grid and on to the winding, overgrown lane that pointed back home.

"Next time," I thought.

Monday, 10th July - Gatton

All that time - prime fishing time - and I never managed to wet a line. But the weather was still cold and wet and so it didn't matter much - I could work without too much of a conscience. This was my first ever visit to the main lake, having been generously supplied with a guest ticket by Roy. I met him at 4 a.m. by the boathouse, and while he took a punt out for the tench I went stalking for a carp. I sneaked along a length of shallows, bordered on one side by big chestnut trees. The caves made by their branches seemed ideal places for carp, but I didn't spot any. I found a beautiful pitch - a little opening between the chestnuts, a soft, mossy bank and a lovely outlook on to a marshy stretch of open ground, with one or two big oaks and then a wood beyond. The water immediately before me looked more like a river than a shallow arm of a big lake.

I caught three nice roach in quick succession, then went to watch the sun rise, from the field of tall grass and mist behind my pitch.

[I'm growing forgetful]. I came back to my rod and went stalking with it almost completely round the lake without seeing evidence of a single carp. I picked up the Avocet on the way back, proposing to fish the mossy pitch with two rods. At the yew branches I risked a bust-up and cast for what I was sure was a feeding carp. But after minutes, the line ran out and I struck into a 2 lb tench!

There were certainly larger fish under the yew tree, but they were all tench.

Back on the mossy bank I had another roach, then one on both rods - except that the one on the Hardy (on the left) put up a dogged fight and eventually turned out to be a good tench.

As the morning went on, I caught more tench - then, as the wind blew the leaves and the sun rose higher, the pitch went quiet and I had nearly an hour's sleep, waking to cast and almost immediately catch another good tench. 4 lb.

The next one, on the Avocet, dived hard into the branches on my right where a big pike attacked it! Luckily I got it in all right and it was only lightly scarred. After that I moved up to an overflow a little way along the bank - the pike had had a quietening effect on the moss pitch.

Casting under the trailing branches I caught a tench from the right (about 3 lb) and then one from the left (about $2^1/_2$ lb). By that time, I'd lost count of the amount of tench I'd caught on this classic tench fisher's morning - but it must have been about a dozen - up to just over 4 lb. My best tench catch ever, and all I wanted was a carp!

Sunday, 16th July - Redmire

After a hot drive into a blazing sun, Clare and I arrived in Hay, at Hawkswood Farm, just before sunset. I helped her take her things into her room that looked out into the wood, then we parted for a few days; she to paint and draw the landscape of the Wye Valley and Black Mountains, me to fish for carp at Redmire.

The sun was behind me as I drove back along the Golden Valley coming down from St Leonard's into Langarren; by then the sun had set and the moon was waxing brighter.

Tom and Roy, here for a visit to repay him for his work last May, were set up and, typically, drinking tea when I arrived. There was just enough light left to see the weed was thicker than at any time in the past. Even the shallows were dense with it. Having a quick glance up there I saw a big carp rolling just off the willow branch opposite - the place where I fished last time. That decided me where to fish this time. Within half an hour I was in position. One rod (the Hardy) had flicked the bait just a few feet to the left of the trailing branch and one rod was all I was going to use. I tossed out a few grains of white corn and then settled down on a cushion, leaning back against the willow trunk.

The moon was bright. Carp were moving in very close. As the moon drifted further down the sky, and a chill breeze began to drift in from the fields behind me, I got into my sleeping-bag and lay back, watching the stretch of water in front of me, framed by hawthorn and willow branches, and seeing even the line from the rod silhouetted against the reflected moonlight. I imagined what it would look like if a carp took the bait and the line tightened. I would be able to see the silver paper rising, like a black flag being hoisted. I dozed, thinking about big slow carp runs, and was almost asleep when a quick hiss had me grovelling for the rod. The line was going out and I struck and saw a big black wave and white ripples spreading out from under the branches. The carp was on and he dived a few yards into the weeds and sulked for a few moments, giving me time to sort everything out and prepare for battle. Slowly, a great pressure came down on the rod and the clutch began to go 'tick, tick, tick', just like a pocket-watch. The weed was thick and I didn't want this fish - which I could feel was a very good one - travelling too deeply into it. So I held on tight and the rod went hard across as I piled on sidestrain (I could only apply sidestrain under those low branches) and tried to stop the unseen, unheard monster. I thought the pressure would bring him up to the surface, but he stayed low and continued to press on into the darkness, still taking line in sharp, powerful surges. It seemed he had gone too far when I eventually brought him to a straining stop. I managed to gain a couple of yards, only to lose it again as the remorseless pull returned, slow and dogged. He didn't seem to be impeded by the weed and I should have realised then it wasn't going to be as much trouble as I'd feared - that it was breaking away easily from the line. But I kept the maximum pressure on, never letting up for a second and eventually, after about four minutes - that seemed like four hours - I felt a last tremendous pull and he was gone. I reeled frantically and the hook came back easily through the weed; it didn't take as long as I'd thought to hit the rod tip. He hadn't gone nearly as far as it had seemed in the dark. If I'd kept a little calmer . . . but then the same thing might have happened whatever the pressure I was applying. I'll blame the bloody hook and leave it at that. It was sharp and not misshapen when I inspected it. But it was a Lion d'Or! Am I a slow learner?

The moon began to curve into the west. A fish took the bait, but bolted as I leaned across the skyline for the rod. I re-baited and just as the moon was touching the trees on the horizon, the silver paper went again and I brought in a small common, about 6 lb, much to his annoyance. At least I managed to wet the new landing net (the old faithful will have to hang on the wall in future).

The dawn was mist-filled and chilly, the sun coming up white through the thin veils that drifted down to me across the fields. The pool was a mass of swirling white. Under the branches a big carp moved quietly, just visible because of the slow whelmings on the surface. He turned across the baited hook, but the line never moved. As the sun climbed higher through the mist, I curled up and went to sleep. I slept for over six hours.

Monday, 17th July

The sun was hot and the day still. Not a carp moved or even showed in the weed or at the surface - and that was very strange.

Needless to say, I never had a chance for a fish, though as I went down to the oaks for my dinner, a big cloud was rising and I knew we were going to have rain. Only gentle rain, though. It lasted for nearly half an hour and all the while, the sky in the west was clear. When it finished and a big rainbow spanned the fields and woods behind me, I was hopeful. But still not one fish stirred.

At dark I waited by my rod under the big willow, expecting the carp to move up as they did yesterday. They did not. I didn't hear a sound all night, nor see a gleam of disturbed water.

Tuesday, 18th July

"I had a 25 in the night!" said Tom, waking me up at 10.0 in the morning.

"Great!" I said, "Let's have a look at it and I'll take a picture."

"I put it straight back," he said. "After all, it might've died in the sack. These old fish you know . . ."

Of course he had the right attitude, but it was odd when I was only thirty yards down the bank that I never heard a thing. He packed up and went home, complaining of a bad back. Poor old Tom.

Roy hadn't had a touch in the Ruins, but he was still hopeful. I sneaked round the lake with my rod, and on the islands came face to face with a big common. It moved out of the weeds just as I let my bait drop on to a little patch of clear bottom under the climbing tree. He went straight down on them and I prepared for the take, which never happened. He slowly turned, with me staring straight down on his broad back and casually drifted away out of sight.

Roy had a chance with crust later as a carp rose up beneath it in the weed-bed. But it didn't touch it.

The moon rose behind cloud, then cleared it and shone down

on the trees round the pool. Their reflections were perfect. After a breezy evening, everything quietened and the night was hushed. The silence by the lake was as if we had found a door and gone through it to another world. After the bustle of the day, the night landscape was like the land of the dead. But the high clouds moved slowly over, and now and then a dog barked, and barked again at its own echo.

My bait was under the big ash on Greenbanks, but the line never moved more than an inch. Roy sat fishing a crust in the weeds, but nothing came up to it, even though a few fish were moving on the top. As we sat, talking in whispers about carp on other planets and other such worldly topics, a big cloud began to rise, like a great foam-capped wave, from the Black Mountains. The moonlight was bright on its crest, but the rest of it was deep and dark.

It was 2.15 a.m. and the coming of that cloud was a good excuse to crawl into our respective bivouacs and go to sleep.

I had a last peep out into the landscape before that, after I'd had a cup of tea and scribbled these last few pages. In the east, there was a break in the cloud and the sky there was a pale, watery blue. The first glimmer of Wednesday.

Wednesday, 19th July

Barry arrived a day early and I was pleased to see him, even though he did wake me out of a dream of carp rolling and swirling and sucking down bread from the surface. Roy, unfortunately, had to leave this same morning and get back to work, but though he hadn't caught a carp he had had an enjoyable visit and did not pack up disheartened. But he stayed as long as he could, for in his pitch big carp were moving and feeding. I had planned to move across to Keffords, but seeing the bubbles rising and the fish rolling not twenty yards from the bank I decided I should move in as soon as Roy moved out. But Barry came up and said he would like to fish there and so I went back to my initial plan.

Roy waved goodbye and drove away at 1.0. I moved some bits round the lake to Keffords, then went on to the island and, with another rod made up, cast out two baits to the carp that were cruising and feeding in the weed-beds. It was the best day yet for feeding fish - never at any time this year have I seen as much movement off the islands. But though I fished intently, I was not confidently expecting a take.

I cast a third rod (the Avocet) out from Keffords into a clear channel between the weeds. Bait was 'paprika-channa' and I was thrilled when, later, from the top of the Island Tree, I saw a big carp feeding over the baited area. Suddenly I *knew* there was real hope for a fish - well more than hope, as I am always hopeful. Let's say I knew a fish would take a bait. But there's the odd thing. Knowing, somehow, a fish would come, I cast the other two rods alongside the Avocet and then, instead of sitting expectantly next to them, I went round to see how Barry was doing!

Maybe it was because I instinctively knew I would lose this next fish and so realised I need not bother much. But that's too defeatist for words. Is the momentum of loss now so unstoppable? There's one thing for certain and that is the fact that no carp hooked when your back is turned should ever be counted as yours - especially if you've gone next door for a chat! All day, though, I had been thinking, "Have I lost 12 or 13 huge carp since my last huge carp - (which was my 13th)? Will I have to lose 13 before I can catch my 14th?" Ludicrous questions, perhaps, but then it was ludicrous the way I'd lost so many big fish, one after the other, when I'd had so little trouble before. I'd tried to discover a reason for all those losses, but I kept returning to the daft idea that it was part of a weird pattern. 13 won, 13 lost. Maybe, obsessed by these absurd thoughts, I knew that I had perhaps outwitted myself and I could never land the 14th without losing the 13th. I was talking to Barry about this and it was only his sympathetic comments that made me think I wasn't as mad as I suspected. He saw no reason why such a pattern shouldn't exist and that, as the pattern was beginning to unfold, there was no reason to dismiss it as pure fantasy.

[Perhaps I was blinding myself to the more likely reason for these losses. Yes, it was all part of a weird pattern - a weird pattern of hook that I once, foolishly, had faith in.]

Needless to say, when I got back to Keffords, in a shower of rain, the silver paper was jammed in the butt ring of the Avocet and the line ran out into the weed-bed. But then I noticed it was still running out. I tightened up and felt a dull throb on the rod top. The line sprang free from one clump of stems and suddenly angled away to the right. Something substantial began to plough forwards. I recovered a few yards; there was a deep 'twang' and the line came free - minus the hook. Thus sank my 13th big fish into the weed-beds and though I punched the ground and cursed, I knew that, perhaps, I would get another chance,or that I'd get a sign that all was now well. Signs! Patterns! 13! The long days of peace have put me into a trance! Am I going to believe anything? Do the carp really meet every third Tuesday of the month to discuss how many rods they're going to smash before the next full moon? It was all too neat - too convenient an argument. I re-cast and, as the night came on and the air cooled quickly after the rain, I zipped up the flap of my bivouac and made a hot cup of tea and then a delicious meal.

At midnight, after clearing a few bits away, I got into my sleeping-bag, read a fishing story, then blew out the candle and immediately fell into a deep, luxurious sleep.

Thursday, 20th July

I was woken at 3.30 a.m. by Barry. Even in the half dark of early dawn I could see his expression of glee.

"I've cracked it!" he said.

He certainly had cracked it, and broken through the door into the club of Redmire carp catchers with his first big fish - and it weighed 30 lb exactly! As soon as he told me it was a leather carp I was eager to see if it was the same fish I'd caught five years earlier at 27 lb 6 oz. It looked a fairly old fish then and it would be encouraging, if Barry's *was* the same one, that it had put on 2 ½ lb instead of 'going back' as all old carp do. It would confirm the suspicion I've had that even the most ancient members of the Redmire colony have waxed fatter since the drought summer of '76. We went round to the oaks to check the weight. Straight away I identified it as 'my' fish. The weight was as Barry had claimed.

Taking it in a sack and lowering it off the dam (we would photograph it when the light grew), I suddenly realised the significance of this big carp. I'd last seen it in September 1973. It was the last 20 lb-plus fish of my early years at Redmire - and my last 20 pounder to date. Since then I'd lost 13 really big carp. Now I'd just put what had been my 13th big carp into a sack. I'd come full circle, though how much more complete that circle would have been if I had caught the fish myself. But that would've been too silly.

I told Barry he had just caught my 13th carp and, far from laughing at my serious tone, he wanted to be assured, given proof, that it was indeed my 13th. I showed him the list at the back of this journal. For a long time we talked about the possible religious, military, planetary, horticultural significance of such a strange occurrence. Why such a peculiar pattern of events and so long and drawn out? Had I successfully landed any of the big fish I'd hooked and lost, this idea would have been knocked on the head before I'd even noticed it. But all those chances were missed and now, looking back, I knew I could never have cheated fate anyway, though I felt cheated at the time. Suddenly, all those lost fish did not seem the least bit upsetting. I'm honestly not grappling for some philosophic excuse, just glad that the pattern of losses had revealed itself so clearly, so definitely. Now, perhaps, I had reached the time when I could begin to succeed again.

[Thus does the crazed mind of the carp fisher descend into numeric nightmares.]

We went back to our respective pitches. I made a cup of tea and lay back on my bed, thinking about all this strangeness and wondering whether it was just lack of sleep (only two hours in twenty-four) that was making our minds ramble and amble into stupidity. Eventually, I fell into a deep slumber.

I was woken about six hours later by Barry - no, I heard him approaching my pitch. I'd woken a few moments earlier and thought straight away that we had been mistaken to be so serious about a peculiar coincidence. Now, as I was thinking that, here was Barry who had just spent the last few hours compiling a list of all his biggest carp - all his 20-plus fish. He showed me the list and described each capture in detail and said he could prove that the list was perfectly correct. Before this trip to Redmire, there were 12 fish on the list. Now there were 13!

Tuesday, 24th July - Abbotsmere

Arrived on the evening of the 23rd, just as the sun was going down over the Black Mountains. The sky was clear and the evening cool. A thin mist crawled across the surface from the fields by the river. And there were the carp, just as I remembered all those years ago;

leaping and rolling off the weed-beds. We (Clare and I) had planned to sleep in the old farmhouse and I would fish in the evenings at the pool, but the well had run dry and the farmer's wife couldn't put us up, so we set up the bivouac down in the rushes, right by the water's edge.

I didn't fish this first night and we just sat drinking tea, watching the reflection of the twilight, talking about the things we'd been doing.

I woke at sunrise and managed to get up then, though only to have a brief look at the mists clearing on the still pool and the sun above the mountains. A heron was disturbed by my face, poking out of the canvas and he flapped over to the far bank. I stalked round to the willows, but there were no signs of fish and eventually I slipped back next to the beautiful dreamer and slept until 10.15.

When we woke, the sun was high and hot and carp were moving through the weed-bed right in front of us. Though they seemed to be ignoring my stale, yellow-gramms, I guessed a crust might tempt one. So I scrounged a bit from a new arrival at the pool and cast a small fragment not far from a disturbance in the purple flowers and flat green leaves. For two hours nothing happened. Then I had an idea. Why not flavour the crust as I flavoured my seed baits? All I had was some mixed ground spice, but I sprinkled that on a few pieces of crust and tossed them out to see what would happen. Within a few minutes three pieces went down almost simultaneously. I saw one fish gobble the bread down only fifteen feet from me, in a small hole in the weeds. I quickly flavoured another piece of crust, put it on my hook and cast it out. The wind caught it first time and it flew to the left. But the next cast was right. Straight away, the carp came for it, but he turned immediately and I thought he wasn't going to be fooled. However, in a few moments, the leaves began to quiver as he circled in again. Down went the crust, the line pulled tight and I couldn't miss. There was a good splash and he dived and lunged to the right, deep amongst the tough stems of bistort. I let him go, then held him hard and the rod curved over and throbbed and the fish came up and thrashed the surface, before diving again and surging away once more. But I held tight and when the pull lessened, the fish 'bounced' back and I heaved and got him a few yards nearer. He thrashed and plunged around just where the weed-bed ended at the margin. Clare got the net ready and he exploded away again, forcing me to give line or risk a break. He surfaced, I got him coming once more and this time he didn't get another chance. Clare lifted and he was ours. About 6½ lb of resplendent wildie lay sparkling in the sunlight on the grass - only the fourth I've had here.

We walked to the village after that, across the fields, and had lunch in the pub to celebrate.

Wednesday, 25th July

Woke early, before the sun had risen, and talked about my fist visit to South Wales with a carp rod, nine years before and how I finally got into Redmire three years later. Those three years were so full of beginnings and progressions and if I'd known then where they were going to lead, I might have been more apprehensive about the eventual tremendous, nerve-wracking encounters with monster carp. And here I am again, back at one of the pools of my youth, still in love with it, still happy to fish for its ancient family of carp, even though I know there are no fish here anywhere near the size of the Redmire giants. But a really big wild carp would give me as much pleasure as a really big Redmire carp - so let's hope I find one in the few days we'll linger here. Clare drawing and reading, and me fishing and reading and writing. What a life!

[It's hardly surprising how, over the years, this simple form of existence has

become so genuine a reality for us while, at the same time, it has put so much conventional reality into the realms of fantasy.]

The sunrise was full of intense drama - enormous black clouds above, and vast white chasms opening up over the mountains for the low sun to pierce through. And though the clouds were moving fast, below the mountains a fine mist, bright in the sunlight, gave a delicate look to the landscape, while the sky, in contrast, was heavy and oppressive.

We dozed into the morning. The wind blew up and what with that and the sound of the kettle boiling, I missed the only chance of the day - a twenty-five yard run, which Clare heard as it sizzled off the reel, but didn't recognise.

The sun went down as it had risen, in a sky full of swirling cirrus and upsurging cumulus. The mountains lived up to their name.

Thursday, 26th July

We walked for miles along the river that, after midnight, was loud with the sound of leaping salmon. We lay on the side of a hill and counted meteorites when the clouds parted. Then we returned to the pool and slept soundly through a warm, very dark night.

Didn't wake until after 10.0, when I suddenly had a feeling a carp was on the prowl. But a carp *had* been on the prowl. Checking the rods, I found the line on the Hardy empty of its silver foil. I hadn't attached it very well and it had sprung off as the fish grabbed the bait, so there was no tell-tale hiss to rouse me. The line had gone through one weed-bed and I cleared it from that and found it leading into the next one along the bank. Perhaps the fish was still on. I wound down, but after much pulling and hauling, I reeled in a bare hook.

We had breakfast and decided to stay one more day - a decision that was rewarded by another carp. Not having to pack up at all or leave for lunch so early, we left it until after midday before preparing to go into Hay. Then, when I went to wind in my two rods, I reached for the Hardy first, but then suddenly decided to reel in the bait on the Carpstick instead. I put in the pick-up and lifted the rod and met a dull resistance that abruptly fired into life! Half of me was amazed, the other half didn't seem surprised at all.

He dived to the left, then right, and as he veered left again, along the line of the bistort beds towards the gap between them, I too went left, lifting the rod over the bivouac and a clump of high reeds until I came to the strip of open water where I could play the fish out. I worked him in a few yards, keeping him away from the weed-bed on the right. Then he made a reel-screaming rush away from me, going ten yards before I could stop him. Eventually we saw him in the grey ripples coming into the weeds on the left. I cleared him from them and over the net he came, plunging and splashing. Clare lifted and another Lyswen wildie was safely enmeshed. A beauty; just under 6.

The afternoon seemed perfect for a big carp; but not a touch.

In the evening, heavy rain began to fall. We went to the Radnor Arms for a meal and it was still raining when we came back to the pool at 8.30. But the clouds looked less severe; as they came down the valley, they were breaking up, and overhead, suddenly, there was a great wash of blue. The rods were cast and night soon fell. We had a last mug of tea and, as drizzle began to fall again, at about 12.30, we curled up together like a couple of cats and prepared to set off on our separate dreams.

I was almost asleep when I heard a quick rustle. I burst through the canvas door, and there was the foil, hissing softly at the butt ring. I struck and was answered by a satisfying weight on the line that began to pull away at speed. I got up from my kneeling position and waited to see what would happen. The fish made a surge to the left and I remembered the weed-beds there, so I piled on pressure. He turned and went back the other way. The clutch buzzed and the rod bent double. I went round to the gap in the weeds on my left and could feel the fish was a long way off. The clutch rang again, he dived into the weeds but I got him out. He went through the line on the Hardy and I didn't like that at all. I got him into the gap, the other line dragging behind him (Clare said the silver foil on the Hardy was hissing like mad!) and he dived first left, then right into the weeds on either side. I pushed the net out but couldn't get him in over the mesh. He ran out and I had to pump him back.

Then Clare came on the scene, rolled up her jeans, took the net and like a true heroine, marched into the black water. I could just see a dark shape coming over the mesh, but from her angle Clare couldn't see it so well and missed first lift, making sure of it with the second. The net frame bent as she hoisted it ashore.

We knelt down to have a look at it in the mesh and, in the dark, with just starlight on its flank, it looked like a 9 pounder. But the dark was deceiving and when I got up at dawn to photograph it, it had shrunk to 7 lb. But he was a very solid fish, just like carved wood. A carp from the monastery stew on a Friday.

We were reluctant to leave, but no doubt our tranquil paradise was going to be invaded by weekenders and, anyway, I had pictures to deliver. Also, we've found a little cottage in a wood that we must go and look at more closely.

Phoned Rod when we got home: "Had you caught thirteen 20s by the time you cast for that last fish in your run of three in August '73?"

"Hang on," (he worked it out). "Yes!"

"That's what I thought. That leather was the 13th, then."

"Yes, it was."

Tuesday, 1st August - Newdigate Place

The first visit this year, though I only had three hours to get a carp. The first run came at 3.30 - a hard fighting 2-3 pounder! Then I had a run every fifteen minutes, some to biggish fish by the looks of the waves they made. Most of them I didn't have time to strike: those I did, I missed - until 4.15 when I got an even smaller fish than the first. At 5.0 I had to pack up, with the carp moving and feeding wherever I scattered 'P.K.C.'

Sunday, 6th August - Redmire

A beautiful sunset greeted me as I drove up to the cottages on the hill. I had to stop a while and look. The sky was full of colour and odd-shaped clouds as I sat down in Barry's pitch - number 13 - to discuss prospects. Out in the weeds a big, black shape rolled lazily.

I set up in Inghams but only had the energy to put out one rod before I turned in for the night. I was tired from the drive, and had spent too long talking to sort myself out in the dim light of evening.

Monday, 7th August

It was a warm morning and the sky was blue and full of high, white clouds that seemed too fair-looking and slow moving to promise rain.

"What I'd like is some heavy rain," I said, "though I doubt if we'll get it. That cloud looks promising."

A dark grey mass was rising in the north and coming straight for us (the opposite direction from the clouds yesterday). After an hour, though, we'd only had a light shower, I looked across the barley-field to see if anything else was showing and the field looked white against a purple wall. A thunder cloud was rising. I thought I saw a flicker of lightning but it was only a butterfly passing close by in the sunlight, viewed out of focus against the cloud.

The pool was still, but I knew a wind would soon be on it. In the sunlight, it was a picture of tranquillity, appearing too calm to be disturbed. The willow-herb hung motionless. The only thing to move was another butterfly, a brimstone, going across the pool, close to the surface. It looked like a flame, with its long reflection the candle.

The wind suddenly began to lean into the trees and the water ruffled. The sun went out and the great cloud slid over. I saw a fork of lightning and heard the crack of thunder soon after - ten seconds after. I dived under the canvas as the rain poured down. At times it was so heavy I could hardly see the trees on the far bank. And when the fury of the rain was at its height, I saw a big carp leap, like a salmon leaping in a waterfall.

In a lull in the rain, Barry's float went up and he connected - a 21 1/2 lb mirror which I netted and immediately recognised as one I'd landed in October 1972. (All these old friends returning after years away!)

But another storm was coming and there was hardly a minute to get out and cast. Only when the sun sank lower did the sky break up. A perfect evening. Still, soaking, mild and with one or two carp moving. But I simply don't feel anything. I'm not responding to my surroundings and feel as if I'm half dreaming. Perhaps it's lack of sleep! A fish would cure me . . .

Tuesday, 8th August

. . . It would've done too! 5.45 a.m. and a dull rattling (wet) hissing had me suddenly shooting out of my sleep and grabbing for the rods, still half in my sleeping-bag.

"Lovely!" was my only utterance as I picked up the quivering Hardy. But in my early morning stupor, the order of striking was badly mishandled. I just tightened up and waited until I felt a solid weight on the end. I hardly jerked the hook at all. A big wave appeared on the glass-calm surface as my fish turned from left to right and angled out into the weeds. The rod went over and then he went down, deep. All was solid for a minute, then he growled on the bottom and I got him moving again. He kicked angrily with his tail and I waited for the boil on the top. But there was only a slight ripple and I bent harder to get him up. Something gave and came towards me. But it was only a bloody great clump of weed!

"AND YOU SAID YOU'D GET THE NEXT ONE!"

"Ah! But it must've been a couple of ounces under 20!"

"Bugger you; give me a 10 pounder, I'd be happy."

"Sorry, a 20 it's got to be; though I can't stop a little one coming if you're going to start prissing around with corn."

And anyway, even if it was a 20, it still doesn't make the 13th reappearing on the night of the last 13th any less strange. Barry says he thinks something must come out of the pattern and we'll have to be watchful.

[Perhaps my guiding spirit has changed into a fish of ill omen. Perhaps I will change into a satin tuxedo.]

As the morning progressed, I was only watchful of the things that moved in front of me: the birds, fish, wind and clouds. It wasn't as warm as yesterday. A cold wind was blowing. I saw a fish on the shallows by the outflow and sat there, on the dam, for an hour or two with my float rod. But the wind made things difficult and I had no bites.

Thursday, 31st August - Redmire

For the first time, I made the journey here from the cottage, having to find new back ways and short-cuts. Came via Newbury, the Lambourne Valley and a village that's actually out of bounds to motorised vehicles.

It was a memorable drive and I arrived at the pool just before sunset. Barry was pitched in the Stumps and I had a cup of tea with him and put the net under a lovely little common for him.

We went up to the shallows to look for monsters, but there was little to see as the wind - or rather, breeze - was beginning to veer round from the east too quickly. I hardly had time to set up a rod before darkness descended.

Friday, 1st September

Woke to a cold breeze blowing down towards me from the shallows. The carp, that had been so active the previous day, were not showing themselves at all. Not until midday, when the sun showed faintly through, did I get a good sign that fish were moving. I prepared the Avocet, put on float tackle and crept behind the stump, on the dam. I put on two grains of corn and dropped the bait in the little hole in the weeds, not three feet out. I felt sure there was a chance of a fish. I'd even said as much to Barry, earlier, fishing in the Evening Pitch.

After a while, Barry suddenly spotted two big carp right under our noses, by the float. I quickly put my polaroids on and gasped. Beneath the quill was an enormous mirror, well over 30. It moved along the bottom and the quill stirred. But then I saw its huge, grey bulk turn and swim slowly out into the deeps. The other fish was still there. After a few minutes it went down under the float. "Steady!" said Barry. The float dithered. I got ready. It nearly slid away, but then lay still again and we saw the dark shape heading out across the little bay.

So close! It was like a repeat performance of September '73, at exactly the same spot with another 30 pounder, though that time, of course, I had a better 'hot' bait and more assurance. That essential extra degree of confidence is taking its time returning. Still, when it does, I'll have earned my reward. It's a curious fact, but total confidence is more important than any bait, however irresistible. Just a split second of doubt or anxiety can actually seem to turn a fish away, while absolute assurance often seems to draw carp to me. I suppose my lack of certitude has much to do with loss of momentum. I've lost the habit of catching carp after almost three years of voluntary exile.

As it grew dark, I went again to the dam and Barry fished there too, inspired by what he'd seen. He had his little fishing chair, I had my sleeping-bag, for it was a cold night with a clear sky and I didn't want to get chilly waiting for my carp. So, after I'd cast and folded silver paper over the line, I lay back, staring up at the incredibly bright stars and satellites. One shooting star curved from the north-west into the south-east, leaving an amazingly long trail. One satellite slowly approached from the south, only to burst into an orange glare and disappear, just as it was coming over-head. But not a single carp moved; not until midnight in fact, when a huge splash echoed out across the still surface and we saw the white ripples spread out way up the pool.

A flock of sheep galloped past us, wary of us even though we never moved or made a sound. Owls called, bats passed low. The lines never moved.

At 2 a.m. Barry packed up and left for home. He's had two small carp this week and he seemed happy enough with those. I've only had half a week and no fish yet (see previous notebook), but I'll keep on trying as I've got over thirty hours left, and thirty hours is a long time to catch a carp. I'll just pray for better conditions tomorrow.

Now it's 3 a.m. and the candle is nearly done. The lake is silent on the other side of the canvas. I can hear only three things. The scratching of my pen, the ticking of my watch and the trickle of water at the outflow. Let's hope I hear one more sound at dawn.

Saturday, 2nd September

There was another sound - that familiar hiss, like an angry snake - that woke me instantly even though it only lasted a second. In my sleeping-bag, I lay listening for what might happen next, but could only hear my heart thumping; the fish didn't come back. The cattle woke me at dawn and I looked out of my bivouac to see a calm, blue sky and the rising sun shining on the stubble-field across the still pool. A faint mist glided across the surface. I re-baited and went back to sleep in that lovely morning and didn't wake up again till 11 a.m. (tut tut).

By that time a wind was blowing and the clouds were coming over once more. A carp leapt right in the corner, to my left. And again. A big fish, too. I made some tea, had some bread and honey, then went on to the dam again and put out the yellow quill and two grains of corn. Across the bay I heard a sharp hiss. My silver paper! Curses! But it was only a snatch - I would've made a dash if there'd been a real run. The quill never moved and after a while I knew it wasn't going to. I went for a walk round the lake. Only when I'd gone two thirds of the way and was looking from the tree-top on the island did I see any carp. They were huge too. One a leather, the '13', and the other the '38' mirror, the Bishop. It looked massive, well into the 40s. Two fish. The last two over 20 that I've caught. Another little coincidence. I'd like to catch them again. I couldn't decide what to do. Whether to move across to Inghams as planned or stay where I was as carp were moving close by. I even thought of moving to the Willows. Perhaps I'll get a sign. Until then, I'll stay here by the dam outfall. The carp don't seem to mind me being here and at least I know they're feeding here and that the wind is pushing this way, when it blows.

The wind has dropped now and the pool is still once more. I'll go into Ross for some cockles - maybe I'll find an old chair for my new cottage . . .

No chairs; plenty of cockles though. Got back at 4.0 and I was glad to have nothing else to disturb me. Nothing to do now but fish. I was even glad there was no one to talk to. Talking can waste valuable time and on this perfect afternoon I didn't want to do that. The sky was bright and a warm breeze was blowing into the dam. I fished there and a big common cruised right past me. As the breeze faded, so the cruising fish melted away.

I had some tea and a big slice of a still-warm wholemeal loaf I'd just bought, with some cheese. Then I climbed up into the big oak and looked out across the deep water. There were three huge fish right below me, all mirrors. Got a really good view, and if the smallest was a 30 pounder, and I'm sure it was, then the big one was over the record. I've not seen it before, either. It didn't look like that dark leviathan I saw last October.

I had another stroll round the pool. There were a few large

commons gliding between Greenbanks and the islands and I decided I'd set up there for the evening. But by the time I'd prepared and then cast out the rods into the open water, there was not much sign of any carp remaining. Certainly nothing like the beautiful fish I saw leap twice, just off the weed-beds. The second time he jumped right out of the water. The splash was tremendous. It was a common and a very dark, burnished one.

Slowly, the sun slipped out of sight and the evening began to cool rapidly. I knew my chances weren't great, but I waited patiently as it grew darker. Over on the opposite bank, against the western sky, the rounded top of a post suddenly sprouted a pair of wings, detached itself from the rest of the post and glided straight towards me. As it went past, only ten feet away, the afterglow lit its pale staring face and showed it to be a barn-owl, the first barn-owl I've seen at Redmire. He flew round my head, like a big moth round a flame, and fluttered on to the same fence post I was sitting against. His claws scraped the wood as he peered down at me, then he flew up and sat in the big ash on my left. I could just see him, a white blob, and I knew he was still looking at me. He was obviously - and justifiably - mystified. After a couple of minutes he flew down to me again. I thought he was going to land again on the post, but he veered away at the last moment, circled me once more and finally disappeared into the willow branches over my head. I didn't see him (or her) again.

Two satellites converged on each other. One glowed suddenly. The Hardy had a take; the silver paper stuttered in a way that almost surely said 'eel'. I struck and in came a plunging, writhing snake-like thing that eventually snapped the hook when I'd got it on the bank. Just as well.

Sunday, 3rd September

Again, a couple of short pulls in the night that came to nothing. Eventually woke just as the sun was rising over the hedgerow behind me. The sky was a clear blue, a vague mist floated across the surface, the light was quite hard. I re-baited and re-cast, then went to take a photograph of the dew on the grass.

My watch said nearly 8 o'clock but the light made me think it was wrong and that it must be much earlier.

I made some tea and listened to a piece of piano music on the radio. It finished for the 9 o'clock news; so my watch wasn't fast. The news spoke of life on another planet where strange-sounding beings made even stranger-sounding statements concerning racial and religious hatred, civil wars, economic decline and the beginning of the new football season.

I sat back, sipping my tea and looking out at the glass-calm reflections. A carp rolled not far away and the ripples spread and spread until they'd wheeled past me and gone into the dam. At 9.15, just as I was going to make a second cup, the line on the right-hand rod began to run quickly out. I was over it in a second, trapping the line and waiting for it to draw tight in my grip. It didn't, but I struck anyway, though it was futile. I'd have done better to strike immediately. A big patch of bubbles rose up from where the bait had been. That one was on a cockle, so I re-baited with cockle on both rods and lay back, watching the sun on the leaves above me (and listening to *Carmina Burana*).

One or two clouds began to form over the Black Mountains; little, white, friendly ones. They floated along that western horizon, not coming to cast shadows over me. A quiet breeze leaned into the leaves and the pool quivered. It was a very peaceful morning. At noon I said farewell to the canniest carp colony in the world and headed westwards to meet Clare at Hawkswood.

19th April

Too many demands, too many days of bad weather, too much living (and loving) to do in our new cottage, I couldn't possibly get back to Redmire or anywhere else. Now it's the Close Season, a wonderful time for all kinds of things not associated with fishing, like walking in the woods, working, snake-hunting, eating birthday cake and getting married.

Tuesday, 29th May

I didn't mind missing over half the month in England. In France, on our honeymoon, it was, at least, like May should be. Green, warm, bursting with colour, echoing with nightingales. The last two weeks, back at home, the month has been wet and miserably cold. No desires have led me out to the waterside to watch for my strange friends; I've just been content to occasionally read books about them or trudge happily back through my years-old angling diaries. But today, when I stepped out of the cottage this morning, there was a change in the air. The leaves looked like they were drifting in water instead of quivering in cold air. It was almost humid and everything smelled of spring. The sky was still grey, but the breeze was warm and sweet and, suddenly, the clouds began to lift. So, this evening I went down to the Wells on my bicycle, as a red sun glowed on the fresh beech-woods. The pools smelt delicious. Pure enough to drink.

Deep under the hanging foliage I leant against a beech trunk and heard a carp leap but missed seeing it. I looked round the trunk and, as I hoped, he leapt again; a big carp rocketing up and walloping back. The still surface wrinkled like a face smiling.

I sat on the dam, listening to a cuckoo and watching as carp sucked down floating leaves.

Grey clouds came over again, so I cycled back up the muddy track, then over the hill and down to the cottage. Clare had lit the candles. The kitchen smelt of roasting chicken. The evening was full of summer.

Rod has given me some interesting details of his new 'killer' baits. There is an everlasting jelly he has devised which he has tried on a difficult water and had immediate success with. Also a bait made up of a mix of dried insects and molasses!

"They'll go barmy on it at Redmire," he said.

Bob Jones came to see the cottage at the weekend and he, too, was full of ideas on baits. But his theory is to recycle old and proven methods - like maggots. Having not seen a maggot for seven years and knowing how well they used to take them, it could be a really effective bait at Redmire - as good, maybe, as corn was in the early days. I can imagine myself float fishing in the shallows over a bed of them. I reckon I can see that float sliding away. There are other baits that I may have more confidence with, concerning this recycling theory. I've never caught a carp on maggots, but I've caught them on kidney beans. Corn has been successful ever since I first used it (1972) but it has taken the catches of another angler at Redmire to convince me it is still a serious bait for a big fish. Ritchie Macdonald caught three 20s on corn last year, while I only occasionally used it for stalking and never concentrated on it like he did. Perhaps I'll sit it out longer now. Trouble is, all these bait experiments demand weeks of careful observation and it's fatal to think about more than one at a time.

Season 20

June 1979 - March 1980

Saturday, 16th June - Lodge Pond

The 16th was as inglorious as a war with one army. A cold night, combined with a mass force of carp anglers and a bank like the lake-bed, made sure the usual opening night foursome (Jasper, Anglepen, Dandy and I) were as uncomfortable as we were unsuccessful. Apart from a spot of excitement in the afternoon, when I thought I was stalking carp but discovered I was stalking tench, the lines never tightened. Still, at least I caught a fish - one of the tench broke me in the reeds! I was quite glad to come away. The cottage seemed more of a retreat than the pond.

Sunday, 17th June

Rick (Birtwhistle Ford) and I drove fifty miles through the lanes of Sussex, hoping for some good sport at Pippingford Park, but were turned away at the last by the new owner. At £50 a season, the fishing will certainly be better there; but we can't afford it. Rick hasn't the time to make it worthwhile and I haven't the money - not after £165 for Redmire. We couldn't understand how Jasper, Anglepen and Nick - who'd arrived before us - had got a permit to fish. They're all even more skint than me.

Luckily, I remembered a quiet little carp pool only twelve miles distant, so we drove on through the darkening lanes and came to the farmhouse just as the farmer was thinking of bed. He was a friendly old soul though, even showing us our way through the dark farmyard and down a newly made path under trees to the pool. And what a delight it was to sit down by a silent pool, ringed in by trees and the new night and know that we were the only ones there. We saw rings on the dark water. There were echoing 'plops' and splashes. This was real carp fishing. Alone with the clicking of the bats, the owl's hoot and the sinking of the carp in the lilies.

Nothing came to our rods until the first light of Monday touched the sky. Then Rick woke me from a pleasant sleep under the oaks with a great shout and I ran along the bank with the net to find him bent into a good carp which was wallowing on the surface. After a bit of a splash we got him in - a superb wildie of 8 lb - one of the most splendid-looking wildies I've seen.

As the light increased, I wandered round the pool, looking for a feeding fish. There were bubbles but I didn't manage to tempt one.

It seemed a whole day had passed by lunch-time - seven hours of daylight and it was only 1 p.m. We had a drink in the pub recommended by the farmer (he'd come down for a chat in the morning and, seeing us wondering at the identity of a hawk, suggested it might be, "one of those hawks with long legs that stands very still". It was a good pub, too, The Star at Heathfield, with a garden overlooking a lovely wooded valley and the bitter cool and well kept.

When we came back to the pool, the sun had cleared the hazy cloud and carp were moving in the weed-beds. Within a few minutes of casting my crust from a position in a reed-bed, I had a take which came to nothing. Then I had another good take and draw on the line. I struck and the line broke! It didn't seem possible.

I tied on a new hook and in a few more minutes a carp moved the water around the fresh crust. It went away, but soon returned and the bread went down with a quiet gulp and the line drew smoothly away. I struck and the fish dived to the right and down. I was forced to give line as he pushed his way deeper into the weeds. He stuck for a while, then slowly came back under pressure and broke surface. Only a small fish but certainly a game one.

Rick woke from his afternoon siesta and came round with the net. Passing it to me, I leant out over the edge of the reeds and drew a 4 lb wildie into the mesh.

The evening seemed promising, apart from the small crowd of village boys who, I suppose, must descend on the water every day, as soon as school is finished. By sunset they had all gone though, and we were left in silence with one carp. I thought of the 17 pounder the farmer had told us about. A wildie too!

I'd moved my pitch to the old oak sluice-gate, where the water dribbled away into the wood below the dam. From there I had a good area of water before me and plenty of lilies and weeds to cast alongside.

At midnight, I made my bed on the massive oak planks and fell asleep till after 4 a.m. when Rick roused me with breakfast. One orange split in two. (God, how I wished I'd been more disciplined and packed my tea-making gear instead of just throwing the essentials into the bag and rushing off - as usual.)

I re-cast, baiting with two chick peas and dropping the lead three feet from the edge of the weeds. Rick returned, and during our conversation I mentioned how I longed to hear the rustle of silver paper. "Why don't we get runs here like we would at Newdigate?" I asked. Twenty minutes later, I heard a 'flick-flick-flick' and jumped forward to see the line streaming from the spool of the old Ambidex. A run! I bent down and picked up the rod, reeling and striking, seeing the line cut up through the surface, slanting down into the weed-bed. By the time I was properly balanced, the fish was twenty feet into it and pulling hard. The Mk IV bent over and then went almost flat as the carp thrust deeper and away; the ripples bumping the weeds and rushes. I kept the pressure steady and didn't hurry things. Slowly, it began to tell and I pumped my prize back to the surface. It stuck for a second in the bistort stems and we could see the line going under a small lily-bed as well, so it was a great relief to have everything suddenly come clear and feel the fish gliding in open water. I had it over the net in a moment. Another wildie - a female in spawn. Weight 8 lb or a little over.

We didn't get another touch all morning, though I found a couple of good fish feeding and heard them glide right under my rest.

We packed up at about 11.0 and went for breakfast at Rick's in-laws in Lingfield, earning our refreshment by catching three ferocious pike from the pool in the garden! They had got in via the outlet stream from Wire Mill Pond and were eating the pet crucian carp. We hooked and lost each pike in turn before finally making good second time around! That must be something of a record (the fish must have been starving).

Thursday, 21st June - Johnson's Lakes, Kent

By a roundabout route - a tragic visit to Milton Mount to see how Crawley District Council had destroyed a once magical lake; a delightful detour to the cottage to collect a few essentials, eat a freshly baked pie and ensure that Clare didn't feel like a newly abandoned wife; then eastward, but veering north for thirty miles so I could have a quick look at Longford and see how Ritchie was doing (he was asleep, but I found a middish 30 lb mirror under a leaning alder and eventually got him feeding so confidently on floating crust that I nearly borrowed one of Ritchie's lip-extracting rods) - I arrived at Johnson's just in time to see Rod and Arnold entering the Bricklayer's for their daily infusion.

We sat at a table overlooking the lakes and I thought how much the scene reminded me of those pictures of the Somme during the Great War. It wasn't just the contrast after the wooded seclusion of the wildie pond; the landscape looked completely desolate

- just great gouged pits everywhere, the remnants of years of gravel extraction, the earth exploited so that we might have thousands of miles of motorways to drive on.

Of course, it was a paradise now for a carp - all those acres of pure spring-fed weed-rich water - and Rod had no time for my namby criticisms; he was completely focused on the fish, and on one in particular, a 'high thirty' in the Railway Pit that he'd almost hooked the previous day. In fact, he was so obsessed by this monster that he said he'd woken up last night to find himself crawling along the bank, looking for it. Not sleep-walking but sleep-stalking.

We finished our beers and went over to his pitch where he'd got some things for me: a nice Ambidex Mk 9, a straight Chapman 500 and - an essential part of every traditional carp angler's kit - a six foot ash longbow, with hunting arrows. We immediately set up a black plastic rubbish bag, christened it Kevin (naturally) and began long-distance target practice.

Quite a gallery of bored, but brave, carp anglers came to watch and they applauded when I finally got Kevin straight through the head. Then Rod hitched up a line from the Chapman to the back rack of my bike and, as he braced himself, I roared off down the track at full throttle, with the Ambidex smoking and everyone shouting for me to 'mash him up'. But the combination of split-cane and 10 lb line was just too much for a 4-cylinder 900 c.c. Kawasaki.

Friday, 22nd June

No carp came in the night, though Rod saw his monster again feeding over a bed of black-eye beans. I lost a big fish in the weed-beds at sunrise, and the rudd that followed next cast wasn't consolation enough, even though it weighed 1 ³/₄ lb.

Left at tea-time, as several thousand weekenders began to invade the place. Even Rod said he might have to search for somewhere quieter.

Had arranged to meet Clare at the Epsom School of Art fashion show in the evening, where she would be modelling various surreal and spectacular creations. My arrival in the auditorium, with all its colour, music and females, was a shock to the system - a bit of a contrast of cultures after Johnsons. Clare looked like an international cover-girl. But after the show, and then the fashion department's party, my head was spinning.

Tuesday, 26th June - The Wells

After an early morning of heavy rain, with mist forming over the woods, the sky cleared and the sun shone warmly. At midday I decided to have a look at the carp in the Wells, but as I only had a bit of stale crust for bait I told Clare I'd be no longer than an hour and might not even fish. I wound on some 8 lb line on to the Aerial, tied the Avocet to the crossbar of my bike and set off up the hill.

Coming to the carp pool through the trees, I thought I was going to be lucky and find it deserted - the bank I could see was empty. But there were four anglers sitting under the trees on the north bank. The carp were there. I watched a group of them swimming round the reed-bed. The place I wanted to fish there was already taken - but on the other side of the reeds, the bank, as I said, was empty; so I walked right round the pool, having a quick word with a couple of the fishermen on the way.

"They're not interested in crust," said one. "Maybe they'll feed this evening. 11 lb is the biggest carp I've heard of, so far this season."

I walked round quietly, coming very slowly along the high path above the reeds where I had a good view of at least six reasonable-sized carp. Hidden behind the oak there, I tackled up and attached a small piece of crust on the 6 hook - a crust lightly flavoured with spice. Then, I carefully crept down to where the stream runs into the pool and gently swung the bait out fifteen feet or so, parallel with the reeds and only inches off them. The line lay across a little clump of them that jutted out from the main bed and, seeing a carp close to this clump, I edged the bread back inch by inch until it was touching it.

Across the pool there was a big swirl as a carp turned suddenly under something (another crust?) on the surface. Was it that difficult here? Everyone said so. Anglers fishing all season with only one carp to show for it. But if a carp turns for crust at midday, in open water, surely I was in with a chance where I was fishing, with the oak shading the water and the reeds so close.

A carp bubbled only a few feet from the crust. He was under that reed clump again and as I watched, he came up on an even keel, then put his nose up under the reeds and hung there - pointing directly away from me and at the bait. He moved gently forward. He'd seen the crust but I wasn't prepared for the nonchalant way he just sucked it straight down and cruised on. He didn't even hesitate! I struck at an almost unmissable fish and he made a big plunging swirl which caused the other five carp to do likewise. They all bolted in the same direction - away from the reeds.

The reel screeched, but not for long. The carp seemed bewildered and just wallowed around without getting anywhere. I'd only brought a little net and it wasn't going to be easy, so I called across and a willing helper came rushing round. I moved further from the reeds, but even so, the fish never made a bolt for them. Probably the shallowness of the water there dissuaded him from that gambit. With the net in the water, he seemed to liven up, boring deep and suddenly making a short, determined run and sending up clouds of bubbles from the bottom. I didn't think he was very big. Perhaps 7 - maybe 8. The Avocet was hard over but I wasn't doing any muscling; just letting the carp circle deep and using plenty of sidestrain to keep throwing him off balance. He seemed very stubborn for a 7 or 8 pounder, even though there were no fireworks. I brought him over the net but it was too small and the fish easily dashed off and made a long run. I brought him slowly back and he came into the bank a few yards to my left. I swung him round and wound gently, bringing his head up as he came back over the diminutive net frame. My 'gillie' lifted and the fish sagged down beautifully with the mesh. As the net was swung out I suddenly realised what a good fish he was. It was the depth that fooled me. A clean, nicely coloured and perfectly conditioned mirror pulled the scales at 12¾lb. I had one more cast after that, but as the carp had so completely vanished, I soon packed up and went home for tea, leaving the other anglers scratching their heads. I'd had a fish within ten minutes of arrival and left ten minutes later. As I cycled slowly away I heard someone mutter, "Bloody noddy!"

Wednesday, 27th June - The Wells

Arrived at 11.30 on a warm, bright morning. There were only two other anglers there and the carp, like yesterday, were swimming in full view of them, up by the reeds.

I went round to the same spot as yesterday, tackling up behind the oak again and creeping down the bank to the edge of the reeds. My foot slipped this time, but the carp didn't mind. I cast gently out and let the crust drift up against the stems. The carp were lolling about twenty yards away and one or two came quite close to me, but I got the impression that they knew what I was. They seemed quietly suspicious, and within half an hour every carp had slowly drifted away down the pool until the shallows were deserted.

I wasn't hopeful after that, but I had a few casts for a big fish further along the bank. Futile. Two carp under a branch seemed oblivious to me - and the crust!

I saw some fish near one of the two lily-beds and put a crust on the edge of the first one. Nothing came near. All the action seemed to be in the other bed. I waited for the one or two cruisers to move out of sight before I moved, stepping very slowly along the bank until I was level with the second clump of lilies. I cast and the crust landed on a pad. I pulled it gently off and it floated in a little gap four feet from the edge of the bed.

The carp glided past. One or two went into the pads. After a while, a group of three fish swam quite close to the crust. One saw it and made an immediate, slow swirl at it. The crust bobbed about, settled, then went down with an audible suck - the fish pointing away from me. I waited a second then gently tapped home the hook.

There was a big swirl and the carp went straight down. For a second I was in trouble, with the line trapped round the reel handle, but I freed it just in time, leaning over the boiling water, then releasing the drum and having the carp run out perhaps thirty feet. There was a rubbery friction on the line as I pumped back through the lily stems. The fish came deep under them, then bolted again. The pads waved and quivered. Back he came again, drawing the pads into a bunch as the line twisted round them. At last I got him under just one stubborn leaf and for a while I thought I was going to have to try and net him from there. I eased off, tightened and after thinking everything was lost for a moment, I felt that beautiful sensation of a fish coming free of snags and into open water. Between the two sets of pads, I had an enjoyable display of tactics, but always I had a last reserve of power in the Avocet to turn the carp in the last yards of danger. With a proper net, there were no upsets at the final stage. A dark-blue and ochre mirror. Perfect condition; 18 lb.

Tuesday, 3rd July - Redmire

An unexpected commission meant a delayed start while I finished and delivered a picture for a book about witches. (While I was in London, on Monday, Barry was sitting up the Island Tree, playing in a 25 lb mirror!). I didn't leave the cottage until 11 a.m., going on the motorbike this time, with all my tackle and provisions in the big bag on the back. Taking a route through quiet lanes and avoiding all unsightly towns, my journey probably took longer than it might've done, but all the memories I have of it are pleasant. Finally, I was coming down that last slope (singing) and under the trees by the waterside.

The pool looked exquisite. Weed thick, but not too thick - level height - and the clarity of water like a polished lens. Barry and John had had a quiet two days in spite of Barry's incredible feat of landing a monster from the top of a tree. It was the only punctuation mark in a long, uneventful sentence.

"Oh yes, they've been going down the shallows."

That's all I wanted to know. I'd fish under the dawn willow and keep my eyes on cruisers going into the upper water.

The sun was an hour from setting when I fixed up the Hardy, attached a twig for a float and cast a hookful of corn under the overhanging willow branch. Already I'd seen the bulging ripples of a carp as it moved slowly along the edge of that bough. As I cast there was another movement, coming in from the right. The little twig drifted at half-cock, very slowly, to the left. Within a minute it dipped and I suspected gudgeon as it bobbed back. Then it slid easily away to the right and I struck into a solid something which suddenly lunged once, then, as I applied the check on the centre-pin, dived straight through the submerged tips of the branch and headed into the weed-bed beyond. I stopped it within a few seconds and drew it back and then it made a longer reel-screaming dash. John came along, luckily with waders, and got into the water with the net. Barry called across that he could see the carp in the weed over to our left. I tried to draw it back through the branch, but it wouldn't come. I let it ease back and then, following advice from Barry, John lifted the branch with his net handle enough to make a little gap. I gently drew the fish towards this space and, miracle, it came through like a ship through a bridge, into the little space of open water beneath the branches. I held it from the right, then the left, saying I didn't think it was big. But John said he thought it was "bigger than you think!" It wasn't. A common, as bright as washed gold; just over 8 lb. It was one of the most perfect-looking fish I've ever seen. I took his portrait in the light of the sunset.

Carp four times his size were gliding past like deep shadows, heading up into the shallows. I fished two willows further along and had a carp bubbling right below the float. A good fish, too. Suddenly, from the left and about thirty to forty feet out, a tremendous carp slid gently into view. It really did look like two or even three 20 pounders in a close bunch, but as it came past I held my breath as I realised it was just the one, colossal fish. Never have I seen anything so big in the shallows. A common that couldn't possibly have weighed less than 70 lb. First I thought 50; then, looking at the others, I thought 90! But 70 is probably the more accurate. I remember hooking a carp up there that, even in the clear shallow water, didn't look more than a 'low double'. I couldn't understand how it fought so well and I took considerable risks as I forced the tackle to the limit in an effort to get the bounder in. It weighed 21 lb. If a 20 pounder looks small in two feet of water, how big is a carp that looks like a baby whale?

Two more giants went past, neither of them as big as the first but each one dwarfing the other fish around them. A carp of around 10 lb that went in under my rod point looked so small as to be comical. But even so, it pleased me that an 8 pounder could be satisfying when all these monsters were so close. The first rites have to be observed before the last. (I would estimate the 'twins' as being 50 or 60 pounders!) Those big fish joined with others at the very head of the pool, churning the water to a dull red-grey, and sending up enormous clouds of bubbles. I couldn't get a touch from the big carp feeding nearby, so I moved round on to the little island, right on top of the mass of feeding carp. They were so close, I almost felt the island tremble and my bait was right in amongst them. I waited till the moon was glowing orange in a hazy night sky, then reeled in and went back to the willow. I hadn't even had a touch. But for all those hours I'd been nearly paralysed with anticipation . . .

Wednesday, 4th July

A clear sunrise, chill and misty. The mist, drifting away from me towards the dam, soon cleared but I only woke properly when it was too hot to sleep any longer.

No carp had been evident at dawn, and all through the morning I might have been fishing on a lake devoid of life. In fact, I didn't fish at all. Something had removed my bait in the night without moving the indicator, but I didn't cast again until the calm of the evening tempted the carp out of the weed-beds and up towards the shallows. Once more I went on to the island at the head of the pool and huge fish (but no apparent monsters), moved close by me. Only once did I have a chance. The line tightened and slid away, but the answering strike produced nothing. It was nearly midnight when I crept back to my bed under the willow.

Thursday, 5th July

Barry hadn't had a touch on his baits since Monday. Even so, I thought it was unlike him to suddenly announce he was going home.

"I can't see me getting another one," he said.

It was hotter than yesterday, and while Barry packed his gear, John and I went into Ross for provisions and a pint of ale by the Wye, watching the salmon and shad flashing through the weed-beds.

Again, it wasn't until about 8 p.m. that I made the first cast of the day. But I hadn't been idle during the afternoon. John and I took the boat up in the shallows and there were tell-tale clouds of mud where the cunning fish had fed during our visit to Ross. And how beautiful the water looked as we drifted over the deeps, in the bright afternoon sun, looking down into the tall forests of weeds. I waded out under the overhanging willow branch and cleared a small gap to cast through. My bait, therefore, would land invitingly just beyond the submerged fronds and just before the edge of the weed-bed.

As the fish began to ghost out of their secret daytime retreats, I cast a bait into my new hot-spot, then cast float tackle out to my right. Drifting scum played slow havoc with the lines. I had to reel in the 'gap' bait. I re-cast after changing rods from Avon to Mk IV. A dreadful mistake, as I forgot to check the strength of a little kink in the line on that rod. A perfect cast sent the bait to the exact spot. A few grains round it and I sat back, absolutely sure a fish would come. A carp cruised in and beneath the float to my right. A cloud of bubbles rose, then he cruised quickly away. A big patch of bubbles rose beneath the branch. Monster size bubbles! A carp was right in the gap and, judging from the signs on the surface, he was picking up the trail of grains that led out to the bait.

I could see the line on the surface and I knew what it would look like as it drew tight. It drew tight and hardly had time to flick the silver paper before I'd closed the pick-up on the fixed-spool reel and struck. A big fish made a bulge in the water, heading left, then hard right. The line, tight as it hit the branch, snapped cleanly beneath the surface without even a sound. A vast wave swept across the reflected sunset. Then all was still. I ripped all the line from the spool and chucked it into my bag. I wasn't so much angry as sad, after all the sureness, that I'd lost the carp I thought I'd earned.

Other carp soon began to reappear again. One began bubbling furiously out to the right. I'd missed what I'd thought was a bite on the float, but in the half light I wasn't sure that my eyes weren't deceiving me. Unbeknown to me, the line from that float-rod, lying now on the bank, had caught round a twig and as that bubbler took the bait - as I knew he would - the bite was revealed by the rod bending to the right! Needless to say, I didn't connect. Some bloody demon must have been under the tree this evening. But he was only there until midnight, when everything became easier and I cast my baits nicely, not having them catch in the branches or land on the unseen scum.

The moon shone down, dull and yellow, curving into the west. Carp seemed to be moving all round me, but as the night seemed to grow slightly warmer rather than cooler, I crawled into my bed and lay watching clouds coming across the moon, darkening the waterscape. The glimmering weed-beds gradually sank into a general darkness.

I fell asleep laughing at the thought of me rushing to the rod, enfolded in my sleeping-bag. I woke only minutes later to the hiss and rustle of the silver paper. It proves how acute my ears are to that sound by the fact that I woke before the tightening line tripped the 2-pence piece from the spool and it fell, 'clink', into the little bowl beneath the reel.

Like a monstrous, deformed butterfly, I emerged from my chrysalis sleeping-bag and pounced on the Avon. The line was steadily trickling out. I put in the pick-up and gave a gentle, firm strike and a fish boiled somewhere out towards the middle of the shallows. It seemed an age before I'd brought him quietly in. All the time I'd thought he was going to snag somehow beneath the branches, but the line was free, as the (stupid) fish had gone the clear way out to the right. I got him to the edge of the weeds and could see a disturbance in the dark water there. There was a sudden, plunging splash and he bolted, going again to the right of the branch. I had to get the net ready, then take off my socks, roll up my trousers and wade out into the luke-warm mud and water. The old Avon bent over against the dark sky as the fish went away in deep surges. It must have almost reached the sticks before I coaxed it back. Twelve feet out it turned and, though I tried to hold it off, the reel began to revolve again as I let him run strongly out again. It swirled once, then again, though I saw nothing. I brought it back, shortening the line and attempting to draw it up over the net which was lying in a mess of weed and scum. But it wouldn't come. The rod went back down. Then he pushed away again and I back-wound for a few more yards. I thought this was a good fish, but certainly no 20, even though he was fighting better than a lot of 20s I've landed. Though he was strong and direct in his runs, I was telling myself not to get too excited. I finally eased him over the mesh and lifted the net. Safe at last, I swung another beautiful common carp ashore. No monster, but a satisfying 10 lb (and a bit).

No more interruptions after that and I slept deeply, waking once to see a cloudy dawn and then again, finally, to find the morning clear and hot, but with a refreshing breeze leaning into the willows.

Friday, 6th July

Again the day was spent enjoying the fine weather, but not fishing. A strong wind began to blow in the afternoon - from the south-west and into the shallows. It was warm, encouraging hopes for an interesting evening's adventure.

At 8.0 or thereabouts, slow, humping ripples broke up the delicate little wavelets of the evening breeze. The carp were moving. I tried out a few handfuls of corn under the tree and within barely an hour the fish had found them and were bubbling like frogs. When they stopped, a few more handfuls of corn had them going again and, all the time, baits were in amongst the free offerings. After an hour I had a slow lift on the Avon and struck into a fish that just hung there, and swayed towards the submerged branches. I persuaded him away and, very slowly, he swam to the right, then out into the lake as John came running up with the net.I slowed him in the sparse weed-beds, twenty yards out, and turned him for a second, then he plunged and made a determined, slow run. I let him go until he stopped of his own accord, then I tried to ease him back, the Avon bent double and the line stretched through the extreme edge of the big willow branch. Then the hook came out.

Within half an hour - when it was almost dark - all activity had ceased. The wind rushed at the willows and the water gleamed in the dull light of a clouded moon.

Saturday, 7th July

Clare had told me that I could have till the end of the week if I wanted. My 'rush job' was a success and, anyway, today was 7th July, a lucky day (I thought), and somehow I didn't give a jot for my work, successful or otherwise. So while John would leave today, I would fish on in welcome solitude and perhaps have another chance for a big fish.

I woke to the sound of thrashing water. The carp were spawning! And they'd already spawned only two weeks ago. They'll be getting exhausted. However, though the noise was such that I got up before sunrise to watch the commotion, the whole pool didn't explode. A lot of carp, big, very big, small and medium, were involved, but by midday, an hour after John had left, activity was definitely decreasing. One or two carp even moved on to the shallows to feed - and that's the first time this week they've done so in the daytime.

At 3.0 I was even fishing(!) - on the roots in the shallows, a quill riding just beyond the bank of scum and a hookful of corn. But more and more very big carp were moving past me and up to the very head of the pool, bubbling and clouding the water. It reminded me of that Saturday six years ago - though that time the fish had an appetite because they were building up to spawning. I even had a can of the same brand broad beans as 1973. Could it work again - a broad bean amongst bubbling monsters? Within minutes I had opened the can and was creeping round the little island at the edge of the shallows. I had the 'heavy gear': Mk IV and Ambidex 9 with 10 lb line. Hook was the Mustad Special.

I dropped a bean in amongst the gently browsing carp. A common of between 20 or 30 went right over it, but ignored it. I tossed in one or two free beans and had to re-cast because the drifting scum was dragging my line. The line tightened but there was nothing when I struck. The kink-tailed mirror went down over the bait. I didn't want to catch that fish - big as he was; there were too many beautiful commons around. He didn't touch it. One or two fish were definitely wary of the bait and accelerated when they came over it. I re-cast again with a very small bean and dropped it accidentally on to the scum, then, in a perfect little gap in the weed, I dropped in three beans round it, and after five minutes two commons came slowly, ponderously, along from the right, the biggest one clear enough of the weed and scum to be seen easily. I looked right down on his broad back as he went over the bait. I'd lost sight of the bean under the drifting scum, but as the fish moved on, the line jerked and curved after him, tightening very slowly. I struck and connected. There was a huge swirl, but the water didn't break. The carp span round and, instead of making the expected lunge into the nearby snags, thrust away to the right, out of sight round the island. I heard the water churning as I grabbed the net and leapt in, wading after the fish. He'd suddenly decided what to do and made a long slow run down the shallows.

I splashed after him, moving to the right where the water was clear - there to fight it out. It was a relief to see him travelling away from the worst hazards. I watched the wave furling away from me. The clutch buzzed and I knew, at least, I'd hooked another 20 pounder. But would I land him this time? There was a great, short, thumping splash as he lunged down into the weeds, and the ripples spread as he turned on a long line first left, then right. Another carp bow-waved casually past us, up to the top of the shallows! My fish made a determined effort to reach a floating willow bank and for the first time I applied all the pressure the tackle would stand and just held him off, with a matter of inches to spare. He went slowly out into mid-shallows again, thumping under the clots of weed, the line cutting into them and sliding on past. The Mk IV was double now as the fish gradually gave a few yards. I worked him in and he rolled and looked very dark - a little like my first Redmire '20'. Then he swung round and churned away from me and I had to let him go, on and on until he stopped, grudgingly, and growled around on the bottom. He made an almost unstoppable thrust under the little climbing tree on my right.

With the rod hard over, I swung him round at the last and he churned the water again and made a big splash and pushed away into the weeds. He stuck a while, but steady pressure soon had him backing towards me, until I could feel him free of the silky growth and he swirled on the top. Again he tried for the tree, again I held him off. Again he pushed powerfully away, down towards the branch. With the line making tinny noises, he suddenly gave it up and back he came. I got the net ready, the handle leaning against me as I worked the carp gradually in. I held the rod high, trying to clear it from the scum and weed, and slowly the angle of the line increased until it was almost 45^0 and the fish only fifteen feet from me. A flag of flannel-weed hung heavily on the line half way between rod and fish, but as it dripped away, it lost its weight and the line sagged less.

As the big carp swirled and plunged I realised how dry my throat had become and how my right arm and wrist ached. All the while I had been telling myself to keep calm, take it easy; trying to insulate myself from the thought of losing this tremendous fish. I remembered that, out of all those I'd lost, I'd never seen any of them clearly and at least there was some consolation in that. But here was a great carp, lolling and rolling in the shallows, only a few yards from the net. I could see his huge scales, see the knot of blanket-weed on the line alongside his flank as he turned away again. That great tail pushing away from me; how far away it seemed. Suddenly, I knew I would snap if I lost this fish. It seems incredible, but something deep down registered a sensation of real fear - as if this was truly a life or death struggle. (I wonder, if anyone was looking, what the expression on my face was like.)

The tail flipped up little splashes as it worked away from me, back into the edge of the weeds. The rod went right over and I held it firm and felt him, grudgingly, submit to the pressure. Fins showed on the surface, then the tail again. It smacked the water. I felt the dull 'twang' of the line across the body of the fish, then everything was smooth as he turned towards me and let himself be drawn in. He hung a few feet from the net, the rod quivering. I wound down a bit to save the strain on the tip and coaxed him those last few feet, pushing the net out and down with a shaking left hand. He came almost quietly over the mesh, his head a little to the left. I tried to lift, but couldn't. In a flash, I'd let go of the rod and grabbed the net handle with both hands. The fish gave a little kick as the frame came up around him - up, up, until the handle was bending with the weight. He lay on his side in the bottom of the net. I stood, elated, up to my knees in water, the ripples from the battle spreading away.

I shouted, I laughed, I even sang; wading down the margins to the platform where I pulled myself up through the Woodcote irises and laid the fish down on the wooden boards. I'd felt his weight as I carried him along and I knew he was not just over 20 lb, but well over that figure. He was 27 lb 6 oz on the scales. A male common.

After I'd emptied the water out of my boots, I walked round, barefoot, to get my camera and photograph him. Then I let him go off Keffords. He was ready to go straight away but I kept him quiet stroking him under the belly. (He seemed to like it as he did not bolt away and I didn't restrain him.) He swam slowly off, eventually, and disappeared into the lush weed-beds.

The warm wind dried the boots and socks hanging on the privy roof. I put them back on and rode off to Langarren to phone Clare and tell her the good news. I phoned J.C. too. I wonder if he thought it suspicious that I should catch a big fish as soon as his back was turned.

Back at the pool, one or two carp began spawning again. But I didn't care about them - or the lack of any signs of feeding fish. I made my supper, then went for a walk up to the hay-field, where I looked back at the lake, down in the valley, with a strong evening breeze jostling the trees. Skylarks sang, bells rang from Langarren. The sun went down into clouds of pure gold.

A broad bean went out on three rods, but all night nothing came to disturb me. The dawn was grey, with the odd gust of gentle breeze. For the first time this week I found carp feeding at sunrise. All along the margins, in fact, little patches of bubbles rose, and tails wove patterns in the surface. I dropped my last two grains of corn next to a good fish. But he just disappeared into the weeds when he saw them.

I packed up, loading everything into the big bag and tying it neatly on to the bike, with the rods alongside, slung comfortably down the length of the machine. A shower of rain pricked the still surface as I prepared to leave. But it cleared within minutes and I set off, down one hundred and thirty miles of green roads and lanes, coming, at last, up the final wooded hill to the cottage. Clare was waiting for me - chicken salad and strawberries and cream ready in the kitchen.

Thursday, 12th July

I could have gone to Gatton today for a session with Roy, but I had a quiet couple of hours at the Wells instead. There were the carp, not so many of the larger ones showing today, but still a good number of fish from 7-14, patrolling the centre of the pool and the edge of the lilies. I tried them with crust after my new 'secret' bait had proved ineffective on the hook. But then two carp came up for the loose 'secret' bait. Suddenly my crust disappeared below the edge of the lily-bed, but the line never tightened and though I waited, I didn't get an opportunity to strike. A good carp cruised away into the depths, visibly munching a piece of crust! There was none on my hook!

26th July - not Redmire

The emptiness of this evening is almost unendurable. It was as if the most impossibly complex relationship with some fantastic woman was about to be blissfully resolved - with everything sweeping to a fairytale end - but then, just at the most crucial moment, someone had put a sack over my head and locked me in a coal shed.

Last week I was suddenly aware of an impending ripe moment. Despite the forecast saying otherwise, I knew that the fortnight of blue skies would soon end with a tropical thunderstorm, that this storm would occur at the end of my next week at Redmire and that, as the pool would not then have been fished by anyone for seventeen days, the carp would be frolicking. Furthermore, I was convinced that the King or his courtiers would inevitably reappear on the shallows after the storm and I would only need to cast once.

But while everything seemed to be moving in my favour, fate decided to intercede. First my old van broke its back and I couldn't get a welder to fix it in time. Then my Kawasaki blew its entire electrical system - with smoke pouring out of the headset. (They'll have to import a new loom from Holland.) Finally, when I managed to borrow another motorbike, from Anglepen, and was on my way to the pool last night, there was a sudden terrible roar and grating from the engine. That was the end of my journey.

"These things happen in threes," said the mechanic I called out (after he'd pronounced the bike D.O.I.- Dead On Inspection). I should have cycled. Or hitched. But there was some power preventing me, and after all the ill luck I had to admit defeat.

Now it is Saturday evening - the end of my Redmire rota - and I sit gazing out of my window at the torrential rain cascading over the woods. Everything is steamy, humid, perfect for carp fishing. There is, as I write, a rumble of distant thunder. Further away still, at Redmire, no one is witnessing the night of the monsters as they turn the shallows red with their wild feeding . . .

Monday, 30th July - The Wells

Had supper early today and was finished by 8.15. Clare went up to her studio to continue work, I went out on my bike into the mild, grey evening, along roads still damp from yesterday's rain.

Someone was fishing in the place I wanted to go - the same spot as yesterday - but I saw a carp cruising beneath the big oak, so I settled down there, trying pasta today, flavoured with paprika. A fish rolled twice, right under the tree, but nothing rose for the free offerings. Down the bank, by some old stumps, a good fish rose for a crust in the margins. I sneaked along there with the high bank behind me. A nightjar chirred in the woods on the other side of the pool and a heron went over, high up in the darkening sky.

A carp was feeding close in on the bottom and I tried for him with a couple of beans. The anglers who had been fishing in 'my' pitch packed up and walked quietly past me, going home. There were two other anglers fishing on the dam, and as they too packed up, so a carp rose and sucked down a piece of crust in the margins. I reeled in, re-baited with crust, flavoured it and cast out along the bank again. A carp bumped the surface very close to it, moved all round it, but didn't seem to notice it.

Suddenly there was a big, plunging rise over to my right. Then another, in the loose offerings twenty feet in front of me. That nearest fish rose again, loudly, and the dark ripples wheeled out across the dark reflections of the trees. I gently reeled in my crust, found the hook was still firmly embedded, and swung it out fast to the left of the scattering of pasta bits.

The two remaining anglers walked slowly away. I could just see the dim shape of them as they went round and into the trees, thankfully not coming round my way. I saw a sudden swirl out where my crust was (it was too dark to see the crust) and heard the noisy suck. The loose line I held between fingers and thumb of my left hand suddenly came alive and I struck, gently, remembering I was only using $4\frac{1}{2}$ lb b.s. line. There was a satisfying, deep lunge, that hung for a second, then plunged and surged away into the darkness, keeping low. The clutch screamed long and loud. I brought my finger harder against the spool but it seemed the carp must almost be in the lily-bed opposite before it came to a grudging halt. I bent the Avocet hard to the left and the fish suddenly turned, and for a second I thought I'd lost it, so quickly did it come in. Then it dived and turned and once more the clutch rang out.

I reached up for the net that I'd left lying at the top of the bank. The fish was down to my left then, but as I tightened up again, having pushed the net into water, he made another long run, heading diagonally across the lake - though it was difficult to judge exactly its direction as it was still keeping very low and hadn't broken surface once, yet. The run ended with the fish lying heavily on the bottom and I really had to strain the light line to get it moving towards me. I pumped and pumped, and by looking at the rod top I could tell it was still a long way out. I wondered how close to that lily-bed it had reached (judging from the time it took to bring in under the rod tip, I reckon it must've almost got into them).

I swung the rod over to the left as it turned again. I even pulled line from the clutch to make it easier for him as he pushed out for another deep run. Again I had to bring the pressure gradually to bear and then, with the rod well round, the fish stopped and hung, moving over to the left with a 'throb-throb' on the line. It was almost dark now as he came into the margins down by the stumps. I watched the water glistening as he moved slowly along heading out and across again. When he was opposite me I lifted the rod high and he surfaced. I saw the swirls and heard the slow splash, knowing he was almost finished now. I shortened the line, but he lengthened it soon after, going out deep again, but then surfacing just out from the trailing branches of the oak.

Back he came, very slowly, close to the top now. He swirled again, but I held him and watched as a grey blur of disturbed water came in under the rod tip, eleven feet out. He was moving slowly to the left as I reached out with the net. He didn't bolt, as I was expecting. It was very difficult, though, to make out exactly where he was. He was hanging almost still, but there was no pale flank showing and no dark shape of the head pushing above the surface. I missed with my first gentle lift. I saw a furl in the water a few feet to the left, reached out, and when I was sure he was over the ring, lifted again. There was a big splash and the net handle shook. Beautiful, the way a live heaviness sagged into the bottom of the mesh. I dragged myself and the fish up the bank to the path and there I lay my captive down to unhook him. The hold was good and secure, which was reassuring. The carp, in the light of my bicycle lamp, looked beautiful. Almost a fully scaled mirror. Deep mahogany-coloured with a large rounded tail. The pointer on the balance read $13\,^3/_4$.

I carried the dark beauty down the bank again and lowered it gently into the margins. It waddled over the ridge of a mud-bank and then cruised slowly away. I held the beam of the lamp on it until it disappeared into the black depths. Then I packed up and was back at home by 10.40. By that time, the heavy clouds that had been gathering all evening thickened to make the night as deep as a well. By midnight a soft rain was falling again in the garden.

Wednesday, 1st August - The Wells

Went again to the place by the oak tree. Anglepen came with me and fished a few yards down the bank. The light was fading as we cast: a blue, clear glow from behind and above the opposite wood. The water was dark, my rod stretching over it was a single taper-ing stripe of blue light. You only get that sharply defined reflection with a split-cane rod because of the flat sections. Tubular rods become invisible after dark.

Small fish flipped and sucked for the crusts, but no carp moved for them. One big fish leapt under the branches with a sudden smack which rocked the whole upper pool.

By the time we packed up, the trees on the far bank were lit with a soft light from the quarter moon.

We didn't go back to the cottage, where Clare would have been making her bed-time drink, but went instead for an abortive attempt at fishing a windy Frensham Little Pond. I would never have gone night fishing there for my introductory visit. A water like that needs perfect conditions for a first attempt. I would rather have gone to bed, but Anglepen was determined to make a night of it, hoping for a Frensham monster, while I slept on the sandy bank instead, my brolly sheltering me from the continuous stiff breeze.

Thursday, 2nd August

After a futile night and dawn, we came home to the cottage for breakfast and, re-fortified, set out once more. Had a look at the carp in the Wells. They seemed oblivious of the fifty floats of the holidaying horrors who surrounded them. And we'd thought we might get a cast at them! It didn't look the same place as last night. We went over to Lodge Pond and found, to our delight, carp moving in the shallows between the reed-beds. All day we fished for them, pin-pointing our float tackle right next to feeding fish and standing up to our ankles in mud while peering over the reeds. It was hard fishing and it earned us nothing.

Came home for tea after a commiserating drink at the local. The sky cleared of the rain-heavy clouds and the evening looked cool and fair. It only needed that brief two hour break to refresh our energies and restore our will to catch a carp. Confident, once more, we returned to the Wells half an hour before sunset.

A carp rose for a free crust minutes after arrival, down by the deep water at the dam end. I cast from there, Anglepen went under the trees in the corner. Carp homed in on our baits, knocked them, sunk them, broke them up, shook them, but never took them properly. It was dark beneath the trees by the time we finally reeled in, admitting defeat once more.

Monday, 5th August

As a heavy sky began to clot overhead and let fall a fine, hazy rain, I rode again to the Wells, coming down the steep lane, just as the lights were going on in the house by the stream. Hoped against hope no one would be at the pool, but I was unlucky and it was forty-five minutes before the four reasonably quiet youngsters packed up and left the pool for me only. After a cast from both banks, I finally cast from the log on the dam, putting out a fairly long line and watching for pale ripples cutting across the black reflections of the woods. There were plenty of ripples, but they were all from small fish and I was thinking that this perfect-seeming evening, with a brooding, low sky and close, warm air, was not so wonderful after all. Obviously the clear, blue evenings were the ones to choose. But then a big white gash opened up in the reflections. A large carp sucked down a crust. I made a long cast and told myself it must be the last as it must've been at least 10 p.m.

Minutes passed. I half noticed a ripple over to my right, at a spot my crust might have drifted to. Then the line gently tightened and I struck. The rod top throbbed a couple of times. Then went straight. I wound fast and caught up with the fish, coming towards me. It turned and bolted to the right, back down the bank and across the corner of the pool. I let the clutch scream, then applied pressure and up came the fish, thrashing on the surface like a trout. It splashed so much I suddenly had the curious thought that it might not be a fish at all - but a duck! It charged off again and I laughed at my stupidity. A duck!

The rod bent as I gave the 4 lb line all it could stand, stopping the fish after about ten yards. It was a fast, powerful run, but I didn't give any more line. I wound in and brought the fish to the surface under the rod tip. I missed once with the net and it dived down and deep, but I swung it gently back and waited, this time until I could see the vague, dark ripples coming right over the net ring. Then I hauled a thrashing carp on to the dam. It was fully scaled, a common built like a wildie. A rare and welcome fish at the Wells. I let him go, packed up and rode home up the dark lakeside path, the bike rattling over roots, disturbing the sleeping woodpigeons.

Thursday, 16th August - Redmire

Circumstances were against me during the beginning of the week. Too much work piling up just at the wrong time, when over the past month things had been spread out nice and evenly. The last time I was due at the pool of pools, I had no ties at all and could have had the whole week there. What happened that week, as before mentioned, was enough to make Box Hill erupt. Anyway, the old van was back on the road, welded together at the weak point with plate steel and now built like a tank. But, because of numerous silly reasons (a builder and a parcels office at the station) it wasn't till 3 p.m. that I kissed Clare goodbye and set off through the green, grey lanes of that afternoon.

The day had started clear and hot, but now a huge sheet of grey was drawing over, and by Newbury the first spots of rain were showing on the windscreen. After that it rained all the way to Redmire.

Barry was dreaming of a fish that had got away as I poked my head under his brolly and said hello. Apparently the fish had gone a bit daft today. If I'd only got here in the morning!

As it was, I only had time to decide which pitch to fish before the early darkness, under the thick cloud, closed in over the lake. I cast one rod, just off the margins, had a cup of tea and some bread and honey, then went to sleep. I woke in the dark to hear splashing on the opposite bank. Apparently Barry was into a little carp, but it was making some fair cat's-cradles with his lines, by the sound of it.

My silver paper had risen to the butt ring and I checked to see nothing was amiss. It would have woken me had it been a proper run but, well, I had to see! Nothing.

I re-cast and just stood there on the bank, admiring the now unveiled night sky. The stars were brilliant and from behind one or two remaining clouds, a pale crescent moon appeared, hanging over the poplars opposite. Its glow was just discernible on my canvas and on the hedgerow behind me. I tried to sleep again, but though I was tired, I wasn't relaxed. I was thinking about lost fish, regretting not being here a day or two earlier. With the pool to myself (B. didn't get here till Wednesday night), what chances would I have had? Dawn soon, I thought. I would have to be up and watchful, as soon as it was light enough.

A buzzard mewed an hour later and I pushed my head out of my bivouac to see if I could spot it. But it had gone over. The stars were still there, though withdrawing now behind the early blue of the new day. The moon looked brighter in that blue - which was odd.

Another buzzard came over, low. The light was just strong enough to reveal the pale under-feathers. He flew slowly away into the sinking night, as if he was following it. Some gulls came over, also heading west. Then a wren struck up his shrill song and the day seemed to have begun.

Friday, 17th August

I found some big carp bubbling off the islands and then one right in close by the platform, his head down in the bottom of a new, deep-delving bowl. (The carp have made a bowl nearly three feet deep there, where there was only a flat bottom last July.) I went back for *two* rods (silly), and the fish was still there when I returned to the platform. But either he knew, as soon as I put my foot on the boards, that I was there, or else a dabchick disturbed him. He slowly pushed out into the middle of the shallows, just as I was casting. There was no weed there now - in fact the weed every-where has died back by about 85% since my last trip.

I stayed fishing for an hour, watching the white sun come up behind the far willows and finger its beams through a light mist that was building up in its glow. A big carp rolled over, out to the right, and as the ripples spread, so the sunlight reflected from them and sent ripples of light throbbing through the mist.

The odd fish bubbled all morning. A dark carp leapt near the islands and fell back, making a tremendous splash.

I had breakfast, then I had a sleep for an hour or two, feeling relaxed now. Then Barry woke me to photograph a superb-look-ing 11 1/4 pounder. After we'd released it we heard a commotion up in the shallows and, looking across, saw the two resident swans swerving around in panic. We thought they must have disturbed a big carp, but they kept up their wheeling about and we realised no carp would keep them going like that. Then we saw it. A small, zipping bow wave, suddenly appearing a few feet from one of the swans, and shooting straight at it. It was as if a pike were attack-ing. But we saw a brown shape fly up for a second as it struck the swan. The swan swerved again, the brown rat or stoat disappeared. He struck again and we fell around laughing when we saw it was a dabchick!

Battle over, the tiny victor fluttered its little wings and swam as dignified as a dabchick can swim (which isn't very), away from the two highly perturbed white monarchs. *They* had just *lost* their dignity.

Though I had one more 'slight' run, there is nothing to report, fish-wise. I ended up fishing into the sunset, with a float under Bowskill's Tree. But the float never moved.

As the stars came out, bright in the cold, clear air, I made my supper and then went to sleep.

Saturday, 18th August

A pesky moorhen had me reaching for my rod at 6.30 a.m. The silver paper hissed, but it was only that annoying bird swimming through the line. I made a cup of tea, hoping that the grey sky would break and the north wind (it'd been south-west to begin with) wouldn't get up again as cold as yesterday. But I'm not complaining. I'm laughing. No carp, bad conditions, probably the wrong pitch to fish, and I'm still happy to be here; sitting in the purple willow-herb, all my rubbish strewn around my bivouac, my rods alert, and yet as asleep as ever, my pen scribbling down a few messages to read next winter - or next spring, when I'll be sitting by my fire, thinking of the new season.

Had a look into the new delving hole in the Ruins - the loose bits of bait had gone but there were no signs of fish. Dave Bufton, the cowman, came over the dam with his two dogs and I had a chat with him while they dived about after a stoat or a rat, or a mink, that had been taking the chicks off the pool.

"Don't see the carp like I used to," he said. "From up the field there I could look across the pool and with, the sun out, I could see their backs and count them, all along here by the dam. I don't see 'em like that now."

No, the fish have changed their habits - but then they've always been changing their habits, to outwit the fishermen.

Dave went off with his dogs (who had tried hard but hadn't caught the stoat or the rat or the mink) and Barry came round to have a look in the Ruins. He saw one fish and I missed seeing it, then spotted a dark tail in the weed-beds seconds later. But it was all very cool, weatherwise and carpwise. One or two fish had rolled, but nothing like yesterday.

Eventually we had a cup of tea at the Willow Pitch and had a lively discussion about the strange dimensions of the mind and how one is conscious of these things most of all when carp fishing. Barry said he often thought that there were times when a big carp had no hope of *not* getting caught. Not only could you will the fish to the bait, but you felt that you *were* the fish, coming in towards the juicy morsel. Sometimes, he said, he felt as if he wasn't with himself any longer, but had gone out to become part of the carp. Whenever this transfer of identity occurred, a take was imminent. And always, something positive happened. Mostly a fish was taken. I said that at certain moments, one's perception was drawn from everywhere around you and for a brief period you had perfect understanding, complete sympathy, total harmony. When that happened, you could do anything. If a big fish was there, you'd catch it.

It was nearly midday by the time we'd finished philosophising. By then the wind was strong, but, if anything, it was a little warmer. A carp rolled under the oaks opposite and I thought about moving round and having a go. But first, a pee, followed by another cup of tea and some bread and cheese.

Fished off the dam for an hour, facing the stiff wind, but feeling the day definitely becoming warmer. The quill bobbed in the incoming ripples - but I don't think there were any fish near. I intended setting up in the Ash Grove, but the view of large numbers of big carp appearing in the weeds, a long way from the Grove, made me change my mind and detour to the Stile instead. Barry had spotted three huge fish from the alder in the Ruins. I climbed up with him and, through binoculars, had a close inspection of the only monster that remained of those three. Two had been commons, this one was a mirror - the Bishop, last weighed in at 38 lb, and now anything between 40 and 50 lb. Last season she looked over 40, but now she was colossal; tremendous width across the back and with a deep belly (containing spawn?). She dwarfed all the 20s around her . . . But is not *she* a *he*? (Or just a greedy pig!) When it was caught in 1972, Jack Hilton positively identified it as a male.

I put my rods ready in the Stile, then had my supper in the Willow Pitch, waiting for the sun to set before moving in to cast. Barry fished in the Ruins with three rods (and three buzzers).

Lay back on my 'beneath-the-stars-bed', watching them as they grew out of the fading sky. A big flock of rooks went over, making a weird din, like a load of tin cans being kicked around a deep cavern. The resident rooks in the high wood, put up a defensive barrage of noise. I thought there was going to be a battle, but the black squadrons passed over peaceably, heading towards the Forest of Dean.

I made a cup of tea, then got into the bag as a chill was fingering its way down from the fields. I pulled a sack over my bag against the damp, felt myself growing warm and was soon asleep.

Woke at about 2 a.m. to the sound of big, splashing drops of rain. Hesitated for a while, then as the shower persisted, I reeled in and retreated into my bivouac, back down the bank, and made another cup of tea as I waited to see if it would stop. It did, eventually, and I crept back to the rods, re-cast, put my bed down again on the now-soaking grass, and was soon asleep and dreaming once more.

Sunday, 19th August

No more rain. Woke to see the sun just above a misty horizon. The sky was a gentle blue and though the grass and leaves were heavy with moisture, like an autumn dawn, it was a very warm daybreak. I felt optimistic - and yet knew, somehow, my chances were waning.

No fish moved. A wall of high cloud drifted over and obscured the sun. For a moment it looked like the moon as the grey bands thickened across its face. I had breakfast while Barry told me of his missed opportunities in the night. By 10.30 he'd packed up and said goodbye and I moved into the Ruins straight away, taking advantage of the loose bait he'd chucked out after his fishing was over. As he drove away, so, absolutely on cue, two carp appeared out of the weeds and glided across the clear hole that held my float. There was just time, I thought, to save an outright blank. Like a fool, I thought my chances better if I brought up another rod. The disturbance was enough to shy the fish; so much so that I well deserved lifeless water from the time I cast that second rod to the time I parted. But I was lucky; with five minutes left to go, two dark shapes again glided out of the weed-beds. They ignored the bait of the second rod, visible in the clear water, and moved right, towards the little dark clearing where my float lay slantwise, like a pen in an inkwell.

I'd been standing on the old willow-stump and I can't remember now whether I was crouching near the rods or holding one of them. Anyway, the orange-tipped quill swung round from 6 to 11 o'clock and slid smoothly away to the right. I struck, and my nerves tightened with the pull of a strong, fast carp. It plunged into the thick weeds, making the Ambidex buzz. I stopped it easily though and with the rod nicely bent, kept a steady pressure as my fish made short, sharp bursts to the right and left. It was 11.25 and it seemed I had saved myself from the experience of a completely strikeless, fishless excursion. The carp lunged to the right, through two patches of weed. But the line was 10 lb b.s. and I could see and feel now that the fish was only a juvenile. Standing up above the water on the willow- stump, the line angled steeply and the rod high, the carp was soon rolling and swirling, and then safe on the bankside grass. 7½ lb. Not an auspicious capture, but one made memorable by the eleventh hour of the occasion.

Wednesday, 12th September - Abbotsmere Pool

In a high wind, Clare and I struggled to set up the billowing canvas and make camp in our favourite reed-bed. We soon had it ready and Clare put the kettle on while I made up two rods.

Two carp-types came over for a chat. We got on to the subject of Redmire and record fish, as it was twenty-seven years and a day since Dick caught the '44'.

"Chris Yates came near it," said one. "Missed by a couple of ounces."

Clare, making the tea, suppressed her laughter.

"That was just a fluke," I said. "I don't think he'll ever do it again, do you?"

I hoped they'd be terribly loyal towards this Yates person, but they just said, "You can never tell *what* will happen at Redmire."

Thursday, 13th September

All night the wind blew and though it died a little towards dawn, morning still found a fresh breeze.

The lines hadn't moved. I reeled in and we went into Hay. I found a good, ancient fishing book, which I bought to celebrate the 27th anniversary of the record.

We returned to the pool at tea-time and I float fished with a savoury offering that I'd found in the local stores: black pudding.

The sunset was clear and spectacular, but the float never moved.

Friday, 14th September

I woke early to photograph a magnificent sunrise. Then, as Clare stirred and began to demand tea, I cast out a bait on 4 lb line and scattered a few black bits around it.

We had breakfast and had just put our cups away, leaning back to listen to some liquid flute music on the radio, when I heard a sudden accompanying hiss. The (4 lb) line was streaming out as I burst from the bivouac, grabbed the Avocet and struck. The clutch screamed and the fish charged away to the right and out. Clare tumbled out with the boots as I let the carp go, on and on. Eventually, with boots secure on feet, I lifted the rod over the bivouac and the reeds and walked over to the left, to the gap in the weed-beds. I waded out and began, slowly, to bring the fish in. It took a long time as it was so far out. Clare joined me and I told her to get some stones in case the fish dived for the weeds. It did. 'Splash!' I managed to hold it off and the stones did the rest. We saw it turn on the surface and after a few more minutes of plunging to and fro, I worked it quietly over the net and Clare hoisted it up. A brazen wildie was swung ashore and laid on the dewy bankside grass.

Tuesday, 27th September - Redmire

The events of this week will always remain a complete mystery to me. Something happened at Redmire that I have never experienced before, yet I can't really define what it was. Did I see the ghost? Did I hook the King? Did I even cast?

Even Jack the Roadman, up at the Royal Arms, couldn't explain when I tried to describe my quandary. However, he was speechless anyway, as I had just beaten him at shove-ha'penny.

Monday, 3rd October - Wadesmarsh

Went for a couple of hours fishing at this pleasant little pool in the heart of a wooded valley. But I wasn't really prepared, bait-wise and though there were carp moving all round the quiet corner where I sat, my line only twitched once. I packed up as darkness fell, determined to come back the next day and catch a fish. They were so obvious, the way they swam close under the margins, the way they fanned the surface with their tales. They looked easy. And though I saw nothing over 10 lb, it would be nice to have a carp clan nearby which never even gave me time for a cup of tea.

Thursday, 4th October

Arrived at about midday and fished on the opposite side of the corner where I sat yesterday - the corner that is the shallows of the pool. The carp were just lying, waiting for me! I'd brought some good bait this time: chick-peas in paprika. I cast out one pea on a size 8 and 4 lb line, over to the right. The second rod I got out just as a veritable mass of carp came and swarmed right in front of me. I cast a little crust after tackling up with shaking hands. It was taken immediately, but not decisively. The line jerked, I struck and missed. The shoal broke up, but the carp kept near the rod and I was able to continue casting crust until a small wildie rose and took the bait properly. The line tightened, I couldn't miss. I had him over the net in a minute and had re-cast the next, pleased I'd got my first carp from this new water - and my first fish of the month.

I sat back to eat a piece of cheese and had just taken the first bite when the line on the 'chick' rod began to run smoothly out and, oh beautiful, the silver paper hissed aggressively. I struck, and a bow wave arrowed across the shallows. On the 4 lb line, I let the Avon take the strain on a light clutch. But I could get a fair bend in the rod and I had to bend it quite a lot as the fish made a great, curving run, going out in a half-circle and coming in to my left, smack into the reed-bed there. The stems swayed and jerked as I gently eased and hauled. He was coming, he was out! Once out I made sure he stayed out. I could see he was only a youngster, but he was a scrapper. The smallest mirror in years rolled, thrashing, into the net. 3 lb!

I had to wait a while for the next one. The lines tightened hesitantly a few times (I'd discarded the crusting idea) and, once, a fish confidently took the left-hand bait, dropped near that reed-bed. But the chick-pea was hooked badly and I missed an easy chance. I also missed a good run on the Avon. No explanations.

Eventually the line tightened on that rod and just stayed, very tight. I struck and a bow wave headed out again. After a bit, the carp made an amazing run over to the bushes on the other side of the shallows. He nearly got there and I was glad the 4 lb line was sound. This was a better fish, though still no monster. He curved to the left and I had to tighten again to change his mind about the reeds. But he could've made it if he'd been more determined.

Suddenly, the line on the Mk IV tightened for a second fish. "Let go!" I did. I got the net into the water as the carp made another long run and it was nearly five minutes more before I could ease it over the mesh. My arm was aching. Another mirror, about twice as big as the last one. I'd got this one on two 'chicks' rather than the single and it wasn't long before the two peas on the other rod were taken properly and the silver paper shot up to the butt ring. The Aerial was whining even before I got my hand to the butt. With 8 lb line and the Mk IV, I was a match for any carp that swam, but this little blighter was going to make a fight of it anyway. After a reel-screeching run, way out beyond the reeds, he then ran out into the middle of the pool and I just couldn't stop him. I worked him in, eventually, until he was running past me and rolling in the shallow water on my right. He rolled and leapt and dived twice, away from the net, before I could bring him safely ashore. An autumn-hued mirror of about 6 lb. The purple scale, the deep orange of the belly and flank were as pleasing to my eyes as a clear sunrise after a month of grey and rain.

Friday, 5th October - The Wells

Clare was late for the dentist so I had to take her in the van. It was such a perfect, bright blue day, I couldn't just drive up the hill and roll down again. So I put my Avon in the back and Clare gave me some stale sweetcorn to try. I also bought a loaf of bread. I was going to the Wells.

The sun was coming up to 11.30 a.m., just high enough to shine on the northern edges of the pools. The beeches turning gold, glowed like flames against the water that remained in the shadow.

There were the carp, hanging like grey airships in a sky of brown flags. The leaves were lying on the surface in great rafts - perfect for crusting.

I cast out a small piece from the beech cove, out towards the carp that were enjoying the first of the sunshine.

My crusting activities were curtailed though, by the sight of a group of carp feeding on the bottom, in the margins, by the withered lily-bed a few yards to my left. I crept along there and dropped a grain of apricot-flavoured corn on the first fish I saw. It bolted!

Further along the bank were two more carp. I dropped two grains on them and one of the fish took the bait as it sank. The line tightened, then fell back, and the two carp swam leisurely off. Too slow! I should've struck immediately. I cast again, into the remains of the old lily-bed and tossed a handful of grains over the bait. Keeping in the shadow of a beech-trunk, so that the reflected sun didn't dazzle me, I watched a group of carp come over the baited area and put their heads down. I looked at the fine line where it went into the water. It tightened, then fell slack, and a fish swam quickly away.

Within about fifteen minutes, the line had moved twice more, each time very hesitantly. Then a fish really got going over the loose grains. His tail waved a foot below the surface and wrinkled the still, clear water. The line, caught lightly against a floating leaf, suddenly came free of it and cut up through the surface, tightening steadily and purposefully. I struck and connected.

As I stepped out from behind the beech-trunk the water broke. It was all flashing and swirls, and I glimpsed briefly a good carp as it circled on the bottom, seemingly confused for a moment, before it bolted into the few remaining lily stems ten feet out and to the right. It burrowed deep into them and there was nothing I could do. I'd had a chance to alter the course of events right at the beginning, when the fish could have been forced, somehow, to the left. But I let him have his head on the 4 lb line. He reappeared on the far side of the pads and made a tremendous rush down the bank and then out, the line running between the stems all the time.

Another angler came up with my net as I began the slow haul back into the lily-bed. Vertically, the line descended into the waving brown fronds; horizontally, it stretched from the fronds to the fish. Five feet down the carp made another reel-screaming run. I pumped it back, gently and gradually it came into the extreme edge of the old lily-bed, plunging and rolling into the wilted, rag-like leaves. It lay there for a while, then plunged down and I lost sight of it. The line was wincing and the rod was bent almost to maximum. But I couldn't get the fish another inch nearer, and after a few minutes there was a sudden tug and lunge and the line broke. The fish boiled on the surface and bolted away.

"Drat!" That's the first fish I've lost at the Wells. If I'd been more sensible, at the beginning or at the end with the net (reaching out with the handle fully extended), I might have had it.

I might have had another one too, up in the shallows where the floating leaves were thickest. A perfect cast put a tiny piece of crust right at the edge of a leaf-raft. A carp lay in the sun on the other side and after a few minutes it pushed through the little clot of leaves, its mouth bubbling at the surface. I knew it was going to take and it did. There was a big 'cloop', but it didn't take the bait properly. It 'clooped' again and although the line didn't move, I made a quick strike and seemed shocked when I didn't connect. Bloody fool! (Just as well you don't have to take an intelligence test to fish for different species. I'd still only have a licence to catch gudgeon.)

I tried for another fish, but it was far too clever. I let the drift take the crust right over it, but it just turned its head away, resisting any temptation. The crust drifted over to another fish and the cunning one, even though it was looking the other way, turned and swam over to the other and pushed it gently to one side. The crust drifted, slowly past. Then both fish turned and began to swim away. But, somehow, the line from the crust which was floating on the surface, caught 'cunning's' tail. He suddenly put on a spurt and the crust accelerated across the water, catching him up. I watched, fascinated, as a big wave shot away, with the line following. The clutch sang as the carp made an amazing run, eventually coming into the margins on the far bank and churning the water there.

I was surprised the tussle didn't take longer than the seven or eight minutes it took to get that tail-hooked carp back across the width of the pool and into the waiting net. 9 lb. A dark, powerfully built, fully scaled mirror. What a pity it wasn't fairly hooked.

Encouraged by the morning's activities, I returned after tea and an afternoon's 'work' to find the pool silent and deserted of anglers. It was a beautiful evening. The sun was just going down and the beeches were like fires going slowly out. A kingfisher flew past. The carp weren't much in evidence. I tried a crust for a while, cast out towards a movement in the leaves. Then I tried corn under the hanging beech boughs. I had one slow take that could've been a roach - but I think it was a carp and I think I could have hit it if I'd been quicker.

The light faded, the evening cooled quickly. A heron flapped overhead.

Monday, 8th October

Took an hour's break from photographing strange shoes and went back to the Wells. It was a grey, dark afternoon, but warm, with a soft breeze. The carp were lying under the leaves that had drifted into a wide border on the south - west end. A carefully cast crust had one or two grey shapes cruise directly beneath it - but not once did they show any real interest in it.

Wednesday, 10th October

After twenty-four hours of torrential rain the lakes were almost bursting their dams. I went down at last light, under a sky that threatened still more rain, hoping to see some activity in the 'enlarged' margins. The little path at the bottom of the steep north bank was flooded and it was here, by an alder trunk, that I cast. But I sat patiently for three quarters of an hour, the sound of rushing water filling the dark woods, and the silver paper never moved.

Thursday, 11th October

Clare needed a quick lift up to the village, so I put my Avon and net in the van and 'detoured' on the way home.

It was a beautiful morning. The sun bright above white, slow-moving cloud; the valley gold and glistening with falling beech leaves; the water calm and dark-looking, with the carp gently mouthing the surface beneath the leaf rafts.

I fished by the Pillars, casting half my measly piece of crust on to the leaf carpet.

After a while, I noticed more movement to my right, so cast again. More than one carp seemed to move directly below the bait. There was a fair bit of bumping and wobbling at the surface and I picked up the rod, hand trembling. The line appeared to be tightening, very fractionally. I wasn't going to make the same mistake as last Friday. I waited. Nothing happened! Eventually, a gentle breeze began to push at the surface and all the floating leaves began to mass to the left. My bait moved along with the general throng and I had to move it to see where it was. There was only a tiny sliver left on the hook!

I went round to the sunny side of the pool, after casting out corn near a bubbler. Perhaps the carp were moving around the old lily-beds; but I didn't see any.

Clare suddenly appeared on the path above me; she'd been tempted by the fine morning and came to see me on her bicycle instead of working on her new drawing. She sat in a patch of sunlight while I sneaked back to my rod on the other bank.

Carp were moving very close, one mouthed the surface only twenty feet away, while another sucked at leaves thirty feet to the left. I found a tiny, dry piece of crust and cast to the left. The fish dematerialised, so I reeled in, losing the crust on the way. I only had corn left. I put on two grains and delicately cast over the leaf raft in front of me, with the carp a few feet to the right of it. The corn would be hanging, suspended, a few inches below the surface and if the carp would only turn round, he wouldn't fail to see it.

The whole, quiet, yellow, green and brown and blue morning suddenly concentrated into one tiny space - that small patch of floating leaves stirring gently as the carp, having turned round, moved back underneath them. The fine line, lying across the surface, began to pull away, very slowly and gently. It was so deliberate I could hardly believe it.

I struck and the rod top tightened into a fish that just hung in mid-water, lolling and plunging but not behaving as if anything was the matter.

Clare, watching from the far bank, had seen each stage of the event; now she came running round to help me with the netting and, when she reached my bank, the fish suddenly decided something was wrong and made a long run out against the clutch. I worked him back slowly, and he dived to the left, keeping very deep. He kept on the bottom for about five minutes, just circling around about twenty feet out and not making any long runs. A couple of bulges on the surface was all we'd seen of him. Then I managed to get him to the top and he swirled once, making a big hole in the leaf raft, and went down again. His circling became a little slower and wider and I began applying sidestrain with all the strength of the 4 lb line. It soon defeated him, rolling him off course and making him turn and plunge. Clare got the net in the water and, as the fish came in quietly, she enmeshed him without any fuss. A beautiful conditioned and coloured mirror of 8½ lb.

Thursday, 1st November

After one visit to the Wells (during which I didn't even cast), two visits to Forked Pond (also castless), and one biteless afternoon at Wadesmarsh (fishing with cockles), I took advantage of the fine, mild, bright weather and came back to the Wells again.

I arrived at about 11.15. The sun was just beginning to go behind the first light cloud of the morning, but it seemed to be set for a good day; the woods still brilliant, the air fresh, but not cold, and just a light breeze touching the tops of the trees. It was half-term and I was expecting to find some little disturbances. I laughed when I discovered there was no one.

No carp showing, either, though I was expecting them to be down, skulking on the bottom after all the past days of wet weather (but still no severe front). I cast out next to the old lily-bed, baiting with two grains of corn (apricot).

The sun was just beginning to rise above the woods and I had it full in my face, though it wasn't really shining on the margins yet. I waited half an hour, then moved along to the right, casting a single grain on a size 12, out by the, now bare, beech bough. I tossed in a few grains round it, then went for a pee in the trees behind me and decided to go up beyond the tree-line and up on to the high common, to have a look at the view. The sky seemed huge up there, blue and full of fair-weather clouds. I could see, in the far distance, Woolmer Hill, looking like a misty mountain. It didn't seem possible that down below me, in the narrow cleft in the trees, a deep pool was reflecting the sky. From the hill top, no one would have guessed that I'd just left my rod a moment and come up 'for a breath of fresh air'.

The sun was at its zenith and still the line hadn't moved. I'd said to Clare I'd be home in an hour or two. An hour or two had passed.

"I'll just wait till that cloud passes." I thought. It passed, but I couldn't retrieve the bait.

"I'll just have a quick look up in the shallows (maybe a fish will take as I walk away)."

Nothing moved under the acre of beech leaves. Nothing had moved all morning, except for one carp that had turned over in deep water with a sudden loud splash. I walked slowly back to my rod and as it came into view, I saw it was jerking. Had a bird just hopped on to it? No, the silver paper was jammed in the ring. Damn! I ran over to it, seeing the line still taut, and half knowing the fish was still there, I struck and felt lovely resistance, though I was surprised that it seemed so close. Hardly any line had been taken.

For a few moments there was the usual confused suggestion on the end of the line. Something went round and round quite quickly, then, having decided all was not well, it headed out to the left and started an amazing, almost continuous run up the whole length of the pool. I had to follow it, whipping round the leaning alders, abandoning the net, getting a boot-full of water and all the time trying to keep the pressure on, though I didn't have much say in matters with my 4 lb line and 12 hook. Eventually I came to the place where I could go no further: the leaning beech that lay almost along the surface by the shallows. I had to lay the rod over and watch the fine line as it cut under the trunk and then dangerously close to it, coming in, so that it stretched along the margin. The carp was somewhere under the near bank, close to the marginal reeds, but there was no visible disturbance in the water. He was still well down on the bottom; there hadn't even been a ripple yet.

Thankfully, the fish moved out again and went round in a big arc, passing me and starting the clutch going once more. I was towed back towards the net, thirty yards down the bank. I came to a stop between the two decayed lily-beds and got some control over my adversary. There was a big swirl, but then down he went and away, the clutch snarling. He was determined to reach the deeps again, so I didn't try and dissuade him and let him pull me past the alders (round the back of the difficult one, passing the rod round the front of it, from left to right hand).

I was back at the striking point and, luckily, the carp didn't seem too enthusiastic about going under the big beech boughs and towards the dam. He just made a series of long runs across the same area of water and after each one I was able to pump him back to about twenty feet from the bank. Then I saw him, dark and sleek, and, predictably, not nearly as big as I'd imagined. The fine line cut through the surface above him, but the refraction made its angle seem wrong. There was another fish swimming close by, much bigger. I began to increase pressure, feeling the nasty 'twang' of the line as the fish lay, facing away from me, swiping with its tail. It dived for something on the left and I didn't like the sensation on the line, but I got it clear.

A few feet down, it began circling, and I countered its

movements with all the sidestrain I could apply. Twenty minutes must have passed and though the rod hadn't been strained, my right wrist was beginning to ache - especially now, as I increased pressure to get the fish up to the top. It wallowed for a moment, then flapped its tail and went out for a way. Back he came and I got the net ready. But the glare on the water confused my sight as I reached out. The carp plunged away and made another long, long run, halfway across the width of the pool. Then followed the slow zig-zagging return, the rod point always a fraction ahead of his changes of direction as I tried to roll him over. On a rightward swing, I got the angle of pull to bring him almost straight in. He surfaced just off the net. I reached out and led him over the ring, then dropped the rod and lifted.

A beautiful coloured mirror lay in the mesh - the same tones as the fallen beech leaves, rich and deep, strong and warm. He was in prime condition - every fin flawless and with a large tail. He had a pronounced underslung mouth. 10 lb he weighed, bigger than I thought when I first saw him in the water. I watched him swim slowly off, leaving a trail of bubbles on the dark water.

Returned at sunset and cast again at the same place. Something jagged the line after only a few minutes. I felt sure I was going to get another fish. It was a calm, silent evening, warm for November. Warm enough for one or two fish to be 'out' near the surface.

The day ended, the waxing moon rose, misty, over the trees, a heron shouted and passed high overhead. I reeled in and the bloody bait had been snitched - probably in that first five minutes - probably by a roach!

30th January - River Rother, Fittleworth

It's always someone else who arranges my winter chubbing; never myself. Today I'd arranged to meet Roy on the Rother after he'd phoned last week enthusing about a good chub stretch just downstream of Fittleworth Bridge.

A perfect day; mild, bright with slowly drifting cloud and a slight breeze texturing the river. Roy was already fishing when I arrived at 9.30. Two swans flew over me as I walked along the bank looking for him. They passed out of sight, going in opposite directions, and when I looked round there was Roy, sitting by the water - it was as if he'd just sprouted up out of the earth.

"So far no good," he said.

I got my Avon (still tackled up after that carp at the Wells in November) and opened a can of corn. I found a nice little slack just downstream of Roy and tried a single grain, free-lined. But there was a slow turbulence under the alders where my bait lay and it wasn't easy to control the line. Some heavy overnight rain had sharpened the current, though it was nothing to what it must have been a week ago. Judging from the tufts of flotsam on the branches, the water must have overflowed the banks.

The sun broke through a bank of cloud and, with a cool breeze blowing, I decided to get out from the shade of the alder trunks and find a warmer, more sheltered swim. The perfect place awaited me only a few yards downstream. A little promontory, sandy and reedy, jutted out under the high bank. The current swung round it and eddied nicely just below it; the best place to drop a little float and watch it hovering in the slowly turning water.

I sat on the sand, in the sun and out of the breeze and propped my rod on a dead thistle. My hat was pulled down to shade my eyes as the sun was shining straight into my face - warm, spring-like. My float gleamed on the brown water.

I was day-dreaming when I suddenly saw the gleam of the float move an inch, then go out! I saw the line tightening as I snatched up the rod and struck - into a solid, deep-running fish. The clutch rang out and the line cut across the river, towards a half-submerged bush. In midstream, the fish slowed and kicked, diving down and hugging the bottom. I brought it up a foot, then lost a yard of line as it bored down again, sullen and dogged. I whistled to Roy, but, unbeknown to me, he had gone upstream, out of earshot. The fish, that I could only hope was a big chub and not a pike - could it be a carp or barbel? - stayed deep and circled slowly in midstream, coming round into the eddy only occasionally. Eventually I could feel the pressure of the 4 lb line beginning to tell. Up to the surface came a dark, scaled back; then it plunged down again, the rod top throbbing and nodding. I got the net ready and drew the chub over first time. It thrashed once in the mesh, then lay still. I carried it down to show Roy. A beautiful silver, slab-sided chub of $3\frac{1}{4}$ lb.

Half an hour later, with the float drifting almost under the rod tip, it slid purposefully sideways and down and I couldn't miss. Again the fish stayed deep, though this one moved faster and changed direction quicker; I guessed it to be smaller, and on bringing it to the surface I could see it was - though only fractionally. It swirled a few times and dived before I got it over the mesh. Just under 3 lb.

I cast again, but after forty unresponsive minutes, I re-cast into the current and tossed a few grains of corn in after the tackle. I let the float go further downstream before gently tightening so that it would swing into the bank and be trapped in the slow eddy. After a minute it bobbed once and then again. I lifted the rod as the float jerked sideways and seemed to hesitate. One more dip and I struck firmly and hooked a third good fish. It dived into midstream, like the other two, and stayed deep. Every so often it gave a fierce jerk on the line and the Avon wagged. A breeze had sprung up again and it made the taut line whine and sing. Anyone watching might've thought I'd just hooked the bottom and was trying to jerk the line free.

That fish hardly moved for the first few minutes, after its initial run. But then I applied maximum pressure and shifted it into mid-water. It bored slowly away, taking a few feet of line, then swung over to my left. I wound down and tried a bit of sidestrain. It worked and I got the fish up near the surface. Not for long though; there was a big swirl as he bolted away, diving fast and deep. Luckily the clutch was set light otherwise that would've been farewell. With the rod top swaying and taut, I got him circling in close, then coaxed him up. A good chub; the best of the day. He dived again and I let the rod tip take the strain and led him round in a big arc - from the main current back into the eddy. I got the net ready and gently eased him over the mesh. He slid in easily and I lifted him safe and sound on to the bank. Another beautifully coloured, silvery chub in the peak of its winter condition. Just under $3\frac{1}{2}$ lb.

I was quite impressed with this introduction to Rother chub; apart from anything else they're quite the most tenacious, powerful chevins I've ever met.

We went across the fields to the pub for lunch; me to celebrate, Roy to drown his chubless sorrows. But the Swan at Fittleworth isn't what it used to be. It was just a limp reminder of its former, jolly self - as limp as the piece of lettuce I had with my sorrowful smoked mackerel! We should have driven to one of the two other, really splendid old pubs just down the road. As it was, I came out at 2.30 feeling dulled and I only had one feeble bite all afternoon.

The breeze strengthened into a cold wind, and dark cloud came up over the South Downs, from the south-west. But the birds sang as if it were late March, as if they thought there'd be no more frost, snow and flood. Maybe they were right. A sea trout leapt.

Walking back to Roy's pitch I put a big polythene bag in my net and in the half light of 5.30 it looked just like an enormous chub.

"You jammy bugger!" he said when he saw me coming along the bank, weighed down with my great fish. He scrambled up the bank and ran over to see it. Then he burst out laughing. Poor Roy; he had to have something to laugh about! *[It may sound as if Roy Henry Tuckey could be embittered by a blank. Not him! He just bit the heads off a few ducks and broke his rod into tiny splinters.]*

We strolled back to the bridge and a lapwing twisted over, just a black flutter of rounded wings. It cried once and the sound had a cold edge to it, as if that bird at least, knew that winter wasn't over.

2nd February, River Rother

After the pressure of the last few days it seemed a glorious release to be driving down through a brightening morning for a day's chubbing with Rick and Roy. Rick was full of hope as we walked downstream, the fresh easterly wind mild in our faces and the sky clearing of white hazy cloud. Roy was already fishing, sitting at his favourite bend waiting for a bite.

I'd told Rick of the success I'd had last time and led him to the swim below the alders where I said he should fish. After all, he'll not get another chance this season and, anyway, I could explore and maybe find another hot spot. I dropped my quill in a couple of places downstream, ending up by a big bend where the current wound slowly under my bank. A kingfisher arrowed by and the sun was warm - yet I didn't have any strong feelings for any of the stretches of water I tried.

I wandered back upstream - past Rick who hadn't had a bite yet and on to a place where a tree lay in the water over the far side and where an alder - a dead one - lay out across the river from my side.

Just below the alder was a lovely, almost still eddy, formed by the jutting bank and a long raft of branches. Above it, and level with the big tree, was another eddy - a long sweep of the current, back along the bank. I tried there for a while but the float never did anything. Then, after fifteen minutes, I moved down the few yards to fish the quiet, shaded glide. There was no denying my feeling of hope for that small sheet of water.

I fished with corn for a while but there were no bites. Then I decided to take the quill off and fish free-line, with only the three BB shot to hold bottom. I re-baited with a little chunk of luncheon meat Roy had given me and swung the tackle just short of the half-sunk branches.

It was getting cooler, even though the sun was still shining. There was a sharpening edge to the wind and my hands began to go numb. Suddenly, the tip of the Avocet bent viciously over. I struck into thin air. But my hands, curiously, were unaware of their former state, as I hurriedly re-baited and swung the bait out again. The morning had focused itself on the tip of the rod. Again it jagged, again I missed. And, half an hour later, I missed another good chance. By then it was nearly 2 p.m. Time for lunch by some warm fire, with a pint of good ale to uncloud logic's grey sky and restore my optimism. I even beat Rick at darts. Roy did not join us as his optimism was still crazily intact.

Back at the river, a thin grey cloud cover had now obscured the sun and the wind felt even colder. Roy, so confident and sure of a fish over his 'lunch break', still had nothing to report. I cast back into the slack, lying now against a tussock so I'd be out of the wind. With rod in one hand and a loop of line feeling for bites in the other, I closed my eyes, sensing a slight dulling of my perception. The short nights of the past week were in league with the beer of the past hour. It felt as if a warm blanket had been thrown over me.

I only slept for a minute or so - my hands hadn't moved, the rod was in the same position. I drew in the bait and swung it out further so that it dropped just at the edge of the midstream current. I felt suddenly alert and purposeful. The line's angle steepened from the tip as the bait settled - then drew smoothly tight again, drawing the tip over determinedly to the left. I followed the direction of the pull with the rod, wanting to give the fish plenty of time, and the line continued to tighten - unlike the last three bites. I struck and the Avocet bent over deliciously. I stood up and the fish did a quick circuit of the eddy, then dashed out into the current and downstream. The centre-pin whined. God! This is a fast one. Maybe it's not a chub. Maybe it's a sea trout. I put the check on the reel and whistled to Rick who was now a couple of hundred yards downstream (he'd given up fishing my 'favourite' swim). He came running across the grass and the fish made another bolt downstream. Then the line began to angle upstream, towards the raft of branches. It was only 3 lb b.s. This could be tricky. I swung the rod over to my left and gave as much sidestrain as I dared. Grattz! The biggest branch quivered in the water and I felt a slight, though nasty scrape. Rick arrived just as I began to ease the fish under the end of the bough and back into the eddy. Phew! I thought that was the end. Perhaps it wasn't a chub or a trout, perhaps it was - curses! - a pike. But then it swirled on the top - a blunt head, a dark tail and a thick body.

"That's one of the biggest chub I've ever seen!" said Rick. It dived under the roots, downstream and stuck for a moment, but only by the force of its own momentum. I coaxed it back and we saw it again on the top before it made a dive into the roots under the rod tip.

"You're going to lose it," laughed Rick, and with the light line, the power of the fish and the abundance of snags, I guessed he might be right. But I got him on the surface again, lying still as Rick reached out with the net. Up came the mesh around the silvery shape and in a second it was safe on the bankside grass.

After making it pose for its portrait, I weighed it, and the pointer of the balance just scraped the 4 lb mark - then hung an ounce or two below. So I called it $3^3/_4$ lb. Cripes! My biggest chub in ten years. But then this was only my fifth chubbing trip in ten years! [*I must return to the River Mole one day.*]

Back in the slack by the dead swan (there was a seriously defunct swan layered into the alder roots, just at the end of the eddy), I cast again and again, and every half hour or so the rod top jerked over. But though I struck instantly, or sometimes slacked off and waited for a continuance of the pull, I never had another connection.

Roy and Rick came round to discuss the state of the temperature and the lack of chub, and as they sat in the grass above me they both saw the rod tip bend viciously. I missed the second best bite of the day.

By six it was almost dark. I watched the last goose fly over, grey and remote in the cold sky, and as we walked up the river a lapwing showed itself, twisting and turning, low over the half invisible fields. It cried out. Then we heard the thrumming of a snipe as it swooped about, somewhere over the fields on the other side of the river.

Sunday, 9th March

After a week of almost going back to the river and being repelled each day by the weather, I finally had a clear sky and mild air; so I ignored the fact that it was Sunday, got my Avocet and a tin of bait and drove down to Fittleworth. Surprisingly, there were only two other anglers on the river and neither seemed to speak much English. I fished the Dead Swan again and had another 3 pounder just after sunset. The evening was so loud with birdsong that it was like fishing in an aviary.

Thursday, 13th March - Redmire

It is the story of this season. Whenever I decide to go to Redmire, something happens. It was no one's fault this time - poor Clare was ill. There was only a bug to blame, but it meant that I would leave a day later than planned, and the day I left, I left late.

Drove through bright skies and sudden storms, arriving at tea-time. The sun was reddening, the clouds flying over from the wrong direction.

After half an hour, I decided to fish under the oaks - where Barry had landed a 26 pounder common last Saturday. Baiting with corn, I cast three rods and quickly got in out of the chill breeze to mould my numb fingers round a hot mug of tea.

The stars were growing as the first carp moved on the surface - just off the Evening Swim. There were one or two swirls that followed with the last light - all on my side of the pool. But the lines were unaffected. The breeze dropped and the night was calm and cold. I expected frost, but there was none. I stood up on the slope looking at the incredible sky; Venus was more brilliant than I've ever seen it and Sirius was flashing through the spectrum like a flickering, multi-filtered lighthouse.

I read for an hour, then slept till dawn, waking with a strong desire for a cup of water. I gulped one down, then slept till mid-morning!

Friday, 14th March

I re-cast only two rods. The wind was up, still from the north, and the temperature was very cold, in spite of the sun and the eager optimistic faces of the primroses.

After an hour, there was a sharp hiss from one of the rods. But it stopped instantly. I debated whether to wait longer and delay my cockle-collecting visit into Ross. I waited - until it was too late to go.

However, I did notice something bob to the surface just off the outreaching oak boughs. I thought it was a small dead carp, but it drifted into the dam wall and began to go 'chink, chink' against the stonework. Incredibly, it was an ancient teapot that had obviously been lying on the pool bed for years. But it must've been upside-down and its little bubble of trapped air had been gradually added to by tiny bursts of methane from the mud. How else could it have suddenly buoyed itself up through ten feet of water? Most peculiar. I picked it out, cleaned it up and took it to a new resting place in a willow tree by the inlet stream. It seemed the right thing to do.

All afternoon, I kept expecting the line to go - even though conditions were appalling. (I wondered if a cockle wouldn't have been more successful.) But I felt a closeness. I knew the carp were feeding. (I threw the 'B' to keep my circulation going). Finally, I spent the last of the daylight on this last day of the season, float fishing from the dam. My chub float bobbed hopefully in the ripples, the wind lessened. But it was still too bloody cold. I even had to do ten press-ups on the muddy track and keep warm and then go for a run across the fields, down to the small pond and back via the strange oak stump. It was too dark to see the float, so I walked back to the oaks. I re-cast the other two rods and had some supper before reeling in again and going down to Langarren to phone Clare. She said she felt much better after a day in bed with all her books and with a good play on the radio.

I went on from Langarren to Langrove, hoping to find Jack the Roadman in the 'Arms'. And there, sure enough, was his warm weather-beaten face. I bought my drink and we sat and talked about eels and trout, carp and badgers and how the poisonous spraying is taking all life from the land.

"You don't see them now," Jack said too often. "The hawks, owls, larks and finches - you don't see them, you don't hear them, like you used to." But he had a lovely tale about an otter hunt here at Redmire. The hunt spotted their quarry soon enough.

"But it wasn't like a little brook, it was too deep and they couldn't get the bugger. They could see him right enough, but he just kept in the deep water and there was nothing they could do."

His one brown and one grey eye hadn't seen the four buzzards his friend had last week. But at least there were still buzzards. Not so many hedgehogs though, and hardly any foxes.

"Get that big bugger," said Jack as he took his leave.

"See you in the summer," I said.

"There's more white Easters than white Christmases," said the landlord as I said goodbye.

Outside in the dark, the pub sign swung in the wind with a sound like a very dry parrot.

Rolling down the slope in my old van and coming to rest by the trees, I thought, "So what if I don't get a carp - at least I'm enjoying being here, at least I made a hopeful attempt, at least I plucked the Redmire Teapot from the cold waters; anyway, it was good to survive all that the elements could throw at me, good to have the pool almost totally asleep in a cold dream that even the wind could not disturb. Next time I'm here, the leaves will be full on the trees and the pool will be awake to my every move - and I awake to the pool."

Five more minutes to go. The wind still blows, the water 'lap-laps' against the dam wall. The clock ticks, the candle-flame is still. All the coots and moorcocks are asleep, at last. Nothing moves except the water and the wind. My lines are leading to midnight - but not beyond.

Season 21

June 1980 - March 1981

The Jester Coot

Sunday, 15th June - Redmire

Packed the van (only acquired last Thursday) after breakfast, with Clare ensuring I had all the small things I usually forget, and left at 2.30, after listening to Britten's 3rd Quartet and watching the clouds gently rolling over the woods. The ten year's new Renault purred along, uncomplaining, down the twisting green roads for the one hundred and twenty or so miles to Bernithan Court.

I parked up in the old enclosure - well out of sight from the pool and then went and had tea with Barry and John, discussing the prospects and generally agreeing that things looked promising. The pool was quite free of weed, the fish were moving and the conditions, weatherwise, were ideal.

As we sat, talking in the old pump house that's now our fishing lodge, a very heavy fall of rain began. As it continued I debated with myself whether it wouldn't be better to set up near slightly deeper water than I'd planned to - the rain having a cooling effect on the shallows. I compromised, eventually, and put up my canvas behind the big ash at Bowskills. One rod was prepared and then, after a final cup of tea with Barry in his pitch, I crept back to my pitch at midnight and dropped in a bait (corn) under the overhanging branches.

It was a cool night and I kept well wrapped up in my sleeping-bag - leaping out at about 3 a.m. as the line began to slide through the silver paper. The run stopped as I got my hands to the rod. I waited; but then just re-set the indicator and went back to sleep.

At 4.0 the hypnotic hiss again shot me into the dawn, and this time the line continued to stream out as I picked up the rod. I struck, and a wave went out across the dim, greyness of the water. For a few seconds, I had to shake myself properly awake, and by the time I was fully in control of my senses, the fish was way down the bank to the right, the line going under the big overhanging branch next to me. I wound the carp in to the branch, but it stuck in the submerged twigs and leaves and I had to go and get Barry to help me get the blighter out. A small common: 8 lb. I made a cup of tea - thinking that though it was a mess-up, at least I'd got the first fish of the season - big or small. That always counts for something; usually the first fish of the season . . . Oh, shut up!

The dawn was quite calm, after a restless night; warm as well. We took the water temperature: 67°.

Up in the shallows, I cast for a large carp that was cruising and bubbling just off the platform. The line tightened once - but it was too brief to hit. Fishing up there in the shallows, I began to feel rather tired. The fish weren't moving much either and I had no qualms about sneaking back to my pitch at 8 a.m. and having a few hours welcome sleep.

The wind got up as I was sleeping. Now and again it roused me as it rushed tempestuously into the big ash above me. Rain fell in torrents - but I slept warm and dry under my canvas. A tremendous clap of thunder shook me wide awake and I looked out to see a midday sky almost black with a huge storm cloud. As it passed over and the sky above brightened, the cloud seemed to darken even more; blue-black in the east. Redmire was whipped up into a rippling sea. The water slapped under the roots below me and sparkled in the flashes of sunlight. I thought of another day like this one - though maybe not quite so turbulent - when I'd landed the 40 pounder. The weather couldn't have been more extreme - but huge fish are often stirred by such conditions. I thought that, yet I didn't do any fishing. There were no carp moving over the shallows and I had no desire to set up in the deeper water. I'd wait and see if the wind pushed some fish up the pool later.

I made myself a meal in the pump house and then Barry and John came round and we sat and talked for an hour about the monsters we'd seen and the possible weights of some of those huge fish.

The sun was shining and the wind had lessened slightly; now just a strong, steady breeze. At about 8.30 we went back to our respective pitches and I saw that another large cloud was filling the sky.

I decided to fish the shallows and rather than use the Mk IV I'd fished with up till then, I set up the Mk IV Avon, proposing to use the Aerial and 8 lb line. But when I tested the line, I knew it was a stupid idea - I'd only got twenty-five yards on the reel! So I put on the Ambidex with 9 lb line, tied on a gold 8 Mustad and, using a float, cast in beneath the first of the willows to my right. After twenty minutes - with nothing but gudgeon moving near the bait - I moved up to the '35' and cast there. On the second cast the float caught against a branch and flew off the line. I didn't bother to put it back. With the drift caused by the (now much softer) breeze, I was having problems keeping the bait stationary - it would be wiser to fish free-line.

I could see some movement coming from the top of the shallows. Big fish were bubbling and sending up clouds of reddy-brown mud. Should I move to the island and drop a bait in from there? Or would I cast from the top pitch - Quinlans, next to the leaning willow? The carp were in range of the latter position, so, after moving up there, I cast two grains of corn (with a small knob of Plasticine on the line to give enough casting weight) out about twenty yards from the bank. There seemed to be five carp feeding and discolouring the water. One was small, three were large and one was colossal. I couldn't identify it, though, because of the mud-clouds.

A big fish, 30 plus, came in from the island, heading straight for the corn. He hesitated over it and I watched the line - ready for an instant strike - but the carp just moved off after a few moments. A large common began to mill about below the floating scum only two rod-lengths out. I dropped a bait near him and after a minute the line shot tight - only to fall slack as I was about to strike. I cast twice more to the edge of the scum, resting the rod on a twig and sitting back on an old willow log. But, even though the breeze had died down to just faint movement of the air - just enough to ripple the shallows - the drifting scum caught the line and dragged the bait about; so I had to reel in again, and was just about to make another cast when I was stopped in mid-swish. That enormous carp appeared again, coming round the trailing willow branches to my left. It was only a momentary pause; then I made the cast and almost botched it. It was like casting into the sun - I lost focus in a fever of anticipation. I thought the line was going into the willow, even though the bait flew true. But a sudden gust of wind bowed the line rightwards and everything fell perfectly. I put the pick-up in and was just lowering the rod when I saw the line sizzling across the surface - just like a chub bite.

The carp had taken the bait on the drop. I couldn't miss and found myself connected to a fish that swirled round, with a thunderous splash and surged diagonally across the shallows. I let it run - having planned a neat move for such a circumstance. I jumped into the muddy margin and splashed across the corner of the shallows, keeping the rod down, feeling it quivering as the line flew from the screaming reel. I had to get under an alder bough that hung right into the water, and managed it, somehow, without mishap. Then I floundered on for a few more yards until I was able to get a good angle of pull and could keep the line clear of the submerged willow. I ended up at the mouth of the feeder stream standing on the remains of the old swan's nest.

A big tail had shown above the surface as the carp charged across the shallows. As I increased pressure it answered the challenge with a tremendous surge of power, making a huge swirl that flattened out all the ripples in an area several yards square. I whistled loudly for help - but there was no answer. "The rats must be asleep!" I thought. I began to shout and the fish made an explosive splash that was heard (I later discovered) right at the other end of the pool. Eventually John answered me.

"What is it?" he shouted. What is it?!? Can't he tell I'm stuck into a giant carp and need immediate assistance?

"Bring a net!"

"Where are you?"

"Right at the top of the shallows!"

The carp, meanwhile, had made the move I'd feared most and was heading back across the shallows towards the big willow branch in the '35'. I piled on pressure and the sidestrain swung it round, so that it was now pointing towards me, and towards the even more dangerous snag - the submerged willow only ten yards down the bank. I felt the bend going out of the rod as the carp moved steadily towards me, heading for that mass of branches. I thought there was only one way to turn it and began to suddenly increase the pressure - hoping it would think I *wanted* it to reach the tree. The fish stopped dead and then with another big swirl, turned in its tracks and headed back down the pool. I let it go - but it didn't go far enough and so I slacked off to a barely bent rod and prayed that John would hurry up. He could frighten the fish away from the menacing branches and send it out into open water again.

I picked up some slimy sticks from the ooze round my feet and threw them into the willow. But the carp just hung, almost motionless, a few yards beyond the mass of underwater boughs. I let the line go slack for a second and felt the fish moving slowly away. I held him after a few yards as he was now going back towards the next big willow, forty yards down the bank.

With much heroic crashing, slipping, cursing and tearing, John finally came round the top of the pool, across the muddy stream and appeared through the trees behind me, puffing and exhausted and covered in mud. He waded out next to me and pushed the net into the water - but it was only inches deep and he had to squelch through the silt for another yard or two until he was far enough out to net the fish when (if) I brought it in.

Suddenly, I felt the carp heading out across open water and I saw a bow wave cutting through the grey ripples, heading for the opposite bank. Without a sound or a word, Barry had come up under the willows and actually climbed into the half-submerged tree, causing the fish to take flight. I swung it round and Barry had a good view of it as I drew it past him. "It's the 38!" he said - but I thought he was joking and laughed, even though the carp was obviously huge. I knew the '38' - the Bishop - must now weigh over 50, and I didn't want to believe we were connected. The implications were too disturbing.

"It's a big fish," said John.

I drew it towards the net and it came into water only inches deep. The inevitable happened - it grounded itself in the soft silty bed. I tried to work it in those few extra feet, but it was like dragging a dead weight and I couldn't risk the danger of a sudden turn of the fish on a line straining at maximum pressure. John, sinking deeper and deeper into the ooze, forced his legs to take him another couple of yards nearer the carp. Then, reaching out, he began to slide the net under the bulk of the wallowing fish.

"Careful," I said. "Go gently - I don't want him to thrash about now!"

He eased the net around the carp until the arms were either side of it - the fish lying broadside on. Then he began to lift. For a moment, nothing happened; he stuck, straining - the mesh didn't seem to be rising up. The fish kicked and I held it tight, trying to keep the head round. John heaved, there was a big swirl and the bend went suddenly out of the rod. For a second, I thought the carp had gone, but it was there - safe in the folds of the big net, with a load of mud, scum and weed.

"Bite the line, John," I said, turning for firmer ground and thinking he would follow.

"You must be bloody joking! I can't even move."

He wouldn't bite the line anyway - saying it wasn't worth taking any chances until we had the carp on the bank. I waded out into the clutching ooze and, taking John's arm, helped him to heave and wrest himself free. We began stumbling back (I felt down the line to see how firm the hook hold was) towards dry land, half falling and staggering under the weight that was in the net.

Barry came running across the marshy field and helped us drag ourselves through the edge of the trees. He looked at the carp as we put it down in the wet grass. It was difficult to see it was a carp - it just looked like a vast black pig that had been rolling in the mud. He estimated the weight.

"53 lb!" There was no emotion in his voice at all!

We each took hold of the net and together carried it over the grass, away from the darkness of the trees so that we could see the monster properly. I can't remember what I was saying. I'd known as soon as John lifted the net in the shallows, that we'd got a record. But I can't remember exactly what was going through my mind. There was a sensation within of huge relief, but also of turbulence - like a wave breaking.

We carefully laid the captive in the long grass and I unhooked it, which was tricky as the hold was very firm in the left-hand side of the bottom lip. I ran for the scales and a pan of water to wash down the silty flanks. We cleaned off the mud and the carp was revealed in all its glory. Perfect condition - and really beautiful colouring. My heart began to soar as I realised that not only was it very big, it was also a classic specimen.

We weighed it, a little unsteadily, and the pointer hovered quiveringly around $51\frac{3}{4}$ lb. I was hardly surprised, yet the shock of seeing a clear record showing on the scales was almost overwhelming. After all these years (and all these diaries!); all those distant dreams that, one day, perhaps my chance would come; all those lost fish and wild outbursts as I lost them - and it all led to this dark-looking mirror carp; a fish I'd caught before, seven years ago; a fish that had seemed too old and tired to ever grow any more. Yet it had grown; it had also become strong and fit, a different carp altogether; a leviathan fit to honour the record books - a monster that I'd called 'the Bishop'.

There were a few moments of awed silence as we crouched round the fish.

"Yatesy's cracked it!" laughed Barry.

I leapt up and threw my hat across the field.

The sky was almost dark, yet over in the west, under the edge of the cloud, a strip of blue showed clear and cool-looking, and in its centre, a thin crescent moon. The breeze had long ceased, the evening was perfectly still and calm.

We weighed it again, more positively, hanging the scales from the bough of one of the big oaks. 51 lb 6 oz. Then Barry and I carried the carp in a huge sack, across the dam to the old punt. Even between two of us, it felt immensely heavy. I stepped in the punt first and the bows nearly went under. It would've been great if we'd gone in then, all three of us! But we managed to work our way out along the length of the boat, then tied the sack securely by both ends and lowered it into the deep water. John appeared behind us and leant on the dam rail, stripped to the waist.

"I won't be able to wear that shirt again," he said.

We drove off to the phone. It was gone 11.0 but I had to call Clare.

"Fifty one pounds!" she squealed.

Then we phoned Dave and the response was exactly the same!

Back at the pool, we made a cup of tea by candlelight and sat, quieter now, with our steaming mugs, re-living the last few hours over and over. In pauses, I stared into the candle flame. Then someone would say again: "Fifty one pounds!"

I finished up Clare's biscuits and we must have drunk seven or eight mugs of tea. We didn't even think of sleeping and just sat talking about the big mirror all night. My mind was still a slow whirl of images: the grey, sullen-looking evening, the few drops of rain, then just the soft breeze and the details of the willows beginning to fade with the sinking light; the slowly unfurling clouds of mud, the big lazy ripples, the four large carp - one of them absolutely colossal; that seemingly impossible, but suddenly easy, fifth cast, the line floating out and just clearing the willow as the breeze caught it; the instant take as the monster took the corn on the drop!

"So many things could have gone wrong," said John, "yet everything went right."

Barry went off for some sleep, just as dawn began to break. I stepped out on to the dam in the dim blue light and a blackbird began to sing from the cable at the edge of the fields. I walked across to the punt. Its dark shape jutted out into the flat grey pool. I stepped into it and felt the sack. The carp stirred. I felt the tail moving from side to side. It was fine.

I slept then (after we'd phoned Tom at 6.30) and didn't wake till around 9.30 when I heard voices next to me. Dave had arrived, full of good cheer and hearty congratulations.

"This has given the place its old magic back," he said. "Do you realise. Everything is starting all over again - it's like Redmire was back in the 50s!"

We brought the punt over to the Willow Pitch and photographed the new record there.

Tom arrived with Doris, and his brittle attitude unnerved me for a moment. He seemed over-worried, afraid that this event would mean more and bigger bids going in for the water. He could only see gathering clouds where everyone else was seeing rainbows and champagne.

The fish went back off the dam - pushing away powerfully into the deep. I went off to Ross for fish and chips and beer and to phone Clare again. When I got back and we'd had the welcome meal, Tom felt much better about it. He'd thought initially that we should hush the entire event up, but that would surely have been impossible.

"Of course we'll have to tell them. And we'll give the story and the pictures to *Angling*."

Everyone went back to their places. Tom and Doris and Dave went off home; I walked up past the barns to the hilltop. Sat in the sun for an hour, letting everything sink slowly in, remembering how sure I'd felt as I arrived yesterday - or rather, Saturday. That's perhaps as exciting as the fish itself. (Take a look at the beginning of this year - I felt it again *then*.) My certainty had been almost disturbing - but then, I'd only felt such absolute confidence perhaps four times before, and on each occasion there was a wonderful easy inevitability in the way events unfolded. So it wasn't exactly a surprise.

Made a light supper, cast out under the ash tree again and crawled into my sleeping-bag. Slept deeply - waking for a few moments at dawn and suddenly remembering the great fish - then slept on into the morning.

Tuesday, 18th June

The breeze was blowing again when I got up for breakfast, but I didn't feel the need to fish, and spent the whole day wandering about humming a merry tune, and no doubt being intensely annoying to Barry and John. But then John began to hum a merry tune when he hooked and landed a mahogany coloured common of $21^1/_2$ lb. On macaroni!

Two days later a quill was snatched suddenly away, as I fished corn from the platform. I hit a carp that bolted right across the shallows and fought superbly on the same tackle I had landed the '50' on. This fish went faster but only weighed 11 lb. A common. It actually ran under a rainbow when I hooked it! I was, though, still in a daze. So was Barry. "It's no good," he said over tea, "I can't fish properly because of you."

Friday, 21st June

Grey, blustery morning - then calm. I packed up at noon, feeling the presence of the pool like an old friend who wanted to postpone the inevitable farewell.

"I'll be back soon," I said as I drove away.

Clare was waiting, happy as ever, when I got back to the cottage. She had a sumptuous meal waiting, and freshly picked strawberries and a bottle of wine, and the telephone off the hook because half the population of the world wanted to know about a fish.

Monday, 28th July

The sun was shining on the woods as I waved goodbye to Clare and rolled off down the hill. Apart from a brief interlude near Basingstoke where I played the Good Samaritan, it was a smooth uneventful journey. The first stubble fields were smouldering in Oxfordshire.

John was fishing in the Ruins and he was in a good mood, having just landed his second 20 pounder of the season. Another 20 common.

"Bring your cup round, I'll make some tea," he said.

I was rounding the corner of the dam and I glanced into the shallow water by the overspill. It was packed with carp! Well, not exactly packed, but there were more fish moving and feeding there than I've seen in years. The very warm easterly was having an effect. Thoughts of tea went out of my mind and I quickly set up the Avon, opened a can of beans (I didn't want to use corn and reckoned a new bait - these beans - might have an immediate effect) and went round to the dam. I dropped the beans in front of a big common, but he didn't appear to see it. I cast again and the kink-tailed mirror went down on it. Quasimodo did not accept the challenge. I wasn't sorry.

One or two big fish were moving in the margin, right under the flowering willow-herb - where the east bank meets the dam. I wandered through the tangle of undergrowth and peered over the willow-herb, looking directly down on the feeding carp. But, because of the reflected sunset, I couldn't see them at all. I swung a bait out and after only a few minutes, the line slowly drew across the surface. I struck and missed. After that, I felt suddenly sure there would be no more chances and 'events', though the fish remained very close and continued feeding. I never had another touch.

I went round to see John for that belated cup of tea and he told me the rest of the details of his previous thirty-six hours. Two more runs he'd had, and one an 11 pounder. It was obviously the effect of his three cane carp rods - Scottie Mk IVs - brought out of retirement after the convincing performance of my collection. He'd even got hold of two original 'claw-arm' Mitchells to go with the one he'd had for years and never used. There were no examples of modern tackle in use at Redmire. No Dan Dare reels; no glass rods. The pool seemed to be responding to the traditional approach of two old timers (John and I are both in our sixth year here).

Great carp began to leap and bubble as night drew on. The moon rose, only a day after full, and, as it did, I made myself comfortable in the mass of willow-herb, wedged behind some alder stumps in my army sleeping-bag. The bait was back at the place where I'd had the half-hearted run. It stayed there all night.

Tuesday, 29th July

In the morning, with the wind still easterly, I thought a float off the dam must work - especially as the dark shapes of carp could be seen moving below the ripples and the floating packweed. I had one or two tweaks, the float bobbing and jerking, but nothing definite. Looking up, now and then, I would sometimes catch the perfect moment when a big carp rose up through the surface and splashed back. They were leaping like polo players.

I moved along the dam and fished the Bush, there, in the side of the punt. Not a touch. John moved into the next gap and had a good bite, using macaroni, but he missed.

I went for a wander and found a big fish with a group of smaller common carp by Wasp Island. I was soon in position (getting through the swamp without even a damp sandal!) and put a small piece of macaroni out into a cloud of mud. (Macaroni was the bait John had been catching - and losing - his fish on: it's a 'Mills creation' as far as the preparation is concerned, and it is going to be another classic, I think, in the tradition of corn.) Nothing happened though. I re-cast with corn and after five minutes, as I was watching the line, a fish slowly moved off with the bait. 3 lb!

I carried on fishing, noticing that the muggy, almost moist breeze had suddenly stopped, and that a dark cloud was rising from downwind. I knew it was going to be a thunderstorm - only a thunderstorm sneaks up on you like that. One or two big drops began to slap down on the glass-calm surface. They stopped for a minute, then, with a rush, the whole pool went white as a great downpour raked across it.

I remembered I'd left my sleeping-bag out and ran to retrieve it in a lull in proceedings. The sky grew even darker and, in a few minutes, the storm proper had begun. I sat in the hut, but couldn't make tea as I didn't have any matches. I ran across the dam and stole two from John, who was sleeping soundly despite the rush of rain and crashing of thunder. I zipped up his bivouac door, then ran, laughing, across the dam as the thunder seemed to roll down after me. It went on for some time and when the last flash had flickered across the blue-black sky and the last, distant boom had echoed away, the fields and paths were left running with water. I couldn't wait to get back to my rod on the island. The wind had changed and swung right round from east to west; the ripples were curving up to the shallows.

A big common, 25 plus, nosed down on a grain of corn, then quickly swam off, as if disturbed. Other smaller fish moved closer, but the bait wasn't touched. Talking to John later on, I said I couldn't decide where to fish and needed a sign. Looking across the pool, a big carp rose up through the rippled, grey surface. It was right in front of the Evening Pitch.

I set up a second rod and even put on a lead! Baiting both hooks with Mac I, I cast one to the right and the other, the Mk IV Carp, along the bank to the left, so that the bait lay right beneath the shadow of the big oaks.

As it got dark, I settled down in my bag, but didn't unfold the brolly. The moon had risen by the time I was asleep.

I woke to a sudden hiss and, in a daze of panic, I grabbed the right-hand rod. The run stopped dead. I re-baited and re-cast, then fell back into a deep slumber, thankful that I hadn't had to do battle when I felt so slow.

When I woke, the left-hand foil was in the butt ring. Curses! I hadn't heard a thing. What a pity that I didn't realise then that it was the quality of the foil that had foiled me. It was too thin - a bloody chocolate wrapper without the cymbal-like properties of cooking foil!

Anyway, the fish was still on when I tightened up. I felt a deep pull from some great depths and I bent hard into it, but failed to move it on an inch. I wound right down, began to pull again and, suddenly, everything came free. The line had broken, right down at the hook.

We had breakfast in the hut. Then went into Ross for provisions. Fished the shallows in the afternoon, casting for fish right up in the scum, at the place where the '50' was landed.

But it wasn't until the sun began to curve down that the fish really began to move in numbers. Hooked a fish at about 8.30 that punched a wave right down the middle of the pool until it was level with the '35' tree. Then the hook popped out. Everything went predictably quiet after that.

Sunday, 17th August

Arrived as the sunset was cut short by an ominous bank of purple cloud. Had a quick look round, noticing the curious opacity of the water - probably algae bloom - but nothing else of note. This milkiness, or rather soupiness, unsettled me as I recalled how the carp often completely disappeared whenever it was evident.

Just had time to tackle up in the Evening Pitch [*or Boathouse Pitch*] - before it was too dark to see. Put one bait along the margins to my left, under the oaks, the other was slightly to the right of straight out. Both rods were Avons - the second one being used for the first time (bought it from Sheet Street). Bait was pink macaroni, cooked this afternoon, at home. Hooks were 6s and I had a $1/2$ oz bomb on both lines. Reels, naturally, were Ambidexes.

The rooks had long settled in their nests by the time I'd finished arranging my bits. Carp began to leap. Slept cautiously! Woke once convinced that a huge cat was purring, then growling behind me. There is no doubt that by a unique combination of unusual elements, unquantifiable elements, the Evening Pitch is sometimes a very odd place to be. And there are now so many weird encounters on record that it must qualify as an S.S.S.I. (Site of Special Spooky Interest).

At first light a quick hiss had me over the rod in a moment. But the run stopped as I picked the rod up. I watched the grey-blue light growing. There was a thin mist on the water. A white planet glimmered above the trees on the far side and the reflection was perfectly still. A bird began to make strange cries of alarm. A cock crowed as the light grew stronger and the stars began to fade. I made myself a cup of tea and when it was properly light, I re-baited both rods.

It was cool, and after sitting for a while, watching, I dozed off and woke, suddenly, out of a dream, the line hissing off the spool. In my bleary state, I wasn't conscious of anything for a while. I just knew I was into a carp and that it was a long way out - towards the Willow Pitch. A wave began to come back to me. There had been no fierce lunge or pull but neither had there been a fierce pull from me. I remembered that I hadn't struck! I just wound to the fish and commenced playing it.

The carp went down deep and I felt everything go solid. I hauled, gradually, but there wasn't a tremor of life. I slacked off and waited. Again nothing, so I hauled again and this time I felt something give - suddenly. In came a load of weed! I suppose I didn't feel too disconsolate. I put the net back up against the tree. I re-baited (the hook had pulled, by the way) both rods and cast again. Then I escaped any after-effects and went back to sleep!

Woke at 10 a.m. for a late breakfast, feeling as if I had a powerful hangover. As I drank my tea, a gusting wind began to drift weed against the lines. The left-hand rod had its line from the tip dragged away to the right. I finished my tea and was just about to

clear the tackle when I noticed the line swinging back to the left.
I just flicked over the pick-up and struck, and was almost surprised
at hooking a big carp so easily!

I felt well into this one as it headed away from the oaks and went
straight out into deep water. In slow, heaving surges it pushed deep
into the late summer weed-beds, and then all went solid. I wound
down and pulled; the (Walker) Avon coiled right round. At first
there was no response, but then I felt an exquisite lessening of
resistance. I began to step backwards, keeping the pressure steady
and firm, and the carp gradually came up from the bottom. There
was a sudden up-swirl about twenty yards out, and in a few more
seconds I saw a dark back. For a minute or so the carp swung back
and forwards, but always losing distance. I had the net ready and
the other rod well down in the water. I saw the dark shape clearly
and thought it was a good common. I'd got my hand round the
net handle, thinking the end was in sight, when the carp made a
heavy plunge and began to run off to my left. I dropped the net
and let him go under pressure. After a while I slowed him, but
then he just thrust away more powerfully, pushing deeper into the
weeds once more. Then all was solid.

"Kratz!" I thought. Right to the net and now he's stuck on the
bottom again!

For a few tense moments I kept the pressure on and it had no
effect. But then - ah wonderful! - the rod began to come back, ever
so slightly, and I kept the pull even and steady again, walking
slowly backwards. He came almost clear, but then dived away
again, though this time he didn't get stuck. I brought him in once
more, the rod absolutely 'U'd. I saw him quite clearly as he turned
and swirled on the surface. Surely it was a mirror and not a common? The back was so dark I couldn't make it out properly. There
was another big splash and again he surged away to the left. I'd
tightened up a good deal by now, but as he got under the bank
and I thought I'd stopped him, he bolted with a tremendous turn

of speed and the clutch screamed. The bow wave shot out into the pool for perhaps 30 yards before I could stop it. Reasonably smoothly, I drew him back in front of me and fought it out at close quarters; the fish moving slowly and doggedly, but tiring now. Over to the right, I brought him up to the surface and he swirled and wallowed there. Working then to the left, I applied gradual pressure from above and up he came, head and shoulders like a rising whale. He came quietly over the net and I lifted smoothly and gently, my heart rising as the mesh enfolded him. He suddenly thrashed with his tail, but it was too late. I drew him to the side and couldn't restrain a 'whoop' of victory. But as I lifted him up I broke the end of the net pole and that could've been nasty; however, all was safe and secure, the carp tumbling in the mesh into the edge of the margin. I heaved it on to the grass and gloated! A beautiful mirror. A good 20 pounder. The flank was dark, the back was dark-blue and the belly was almost brick-red. Easily the most splendid coloured mirror I've caught. Just over 25 1/2 lb on my pocket balance.

I let him recover in a sack, then photographed him and released him from Ash Grove. He went off with a 'whoosh' leaving a cloud of mud and gyrations in the surface that lasted for nearly a minute after he'd disappeared.

The church bells were ringing from Langarren. The sun shone warmly after a morning of showers and wind. I went for a run to clear the system. Looked at the clouds sailing over the Black Mountains, then ran down to the little pond below the main pool. Thought I could see two fish in the shallow water so I sneaked round to where an old gate stands on the bank and there I could see there *were* two fish. Both common carp. One about 7, the other perhaps 14 1b. They were browsing very slowly on the mud, and after a minute I tapped the woodwork of the gate and they went off with a great thumping splash. But they only went round in a wide circle, coming back to their former positions.

Up in the shallows, some big fish were feeding so I took two rods and the net (now fixed) and cast from the platform. The carp definitely seemed to sense my presence, so I moved round to the '50' willow and saw there what I'm sure was my 25 lb mirror, the tip of his dorsal showing as he recovered strength after the strain of battle. Apart from his obvious sleepy behaviour, he seemed OK. He was moving about all right. (It was, in fact, a different, smaller fish.) I cast next to the willow, but nothing came near. I cast on the other side of it, free-lining with one piece of macaroni and tossing a few round the hook. I stood, sure of a take, and it came after fifteen minutes, the line quickly drawing tight and the answering strike sending a fish surging across the shallows. It curved round to the left and made a long run past the '35' willow, sidestrain having no effect. But, after about twenty-five yards, I slowed and stopped it - judging by the angle of line that I might just be lucky enough to avoid having the fish crash into the sunken boughs. I was lucky. The carp swung out, coming past me fifteen yards from the bank. Only when it was nearly in the '50' willow did I really pile on the sidestrain again. I almost came too late with it!

It came in easily after that, but walloped about a good bit when the mesh of the net was up around it. A superb-looking common; perfect proportions. 12¼ lb.

The evening calmed, an hour after sunset. The moon washed its face in the pool and a big carp leapt over on the far side.

Slept better, though twice I woke thinking once more that some large animal was lying down next to me - or on top of me! There was no doubting the sense of presence when I stared into the darkness - yet it wasn't like peering at a midnight badger sett. There was something far more dangerous about the feel of things which first made me cringe, then roar with laughter. This really is a terrific place!

I cast *three* rods at dawn - all MK IVs - but nothing happened until the movement on the clock that I was waiting for. 10.30 - again.

I was reading *Come Fishing With Me* and had just finished the line about 'nature's refrigerator' when a sharp hiss had me leaning for the rod. It stopped, but I struck, and connected as the line tightened the second time.

A fast-moving fish went out along the same line as the '25'. This one was on the new Avon and 10 lb line, so I really crammed the pressure on, lifting the rod high and bringing the carp up to the top. It swirled and plunged, then bolted away, making the reel scream. It made it two thirds of the way across the pool, then came round in a semi-circle (I saw another surface-swimming carp pass under the stretched line) and nose-dived. I should've run backwards, rather than just keep up with him. He speared himself into that thick weed and stuck fast.

After five minutes, with no response, I lay the rod down and watched the line on the surface. It didn't move. I tightened up again, thinking this was bound to be a reasonable fish and wondering whether I should try to get the punt out. I hauled, gently, and stepped backwards. Nothing. But then, as I kept up the pressure, I felt a tremor of life. I wound down and hauled again. Something gave a foot or so - a beautiful sensation. Then I got another few inches, and in a minute or so I had a great weight suddenly coming free. Up to the surface came a mass of weed.

"Oh no!" I thought, thinking it was only weed. But then I felt the 'throb-throb' of a tail and the weed began to head to the right. I swung it all in towards me and was surprised at the small scales on the flank as I drew the fish into the net. Small scales, 'small' carp. A common of 11 lb. But I was still happy with my catch, even though I'd been sure all along this was going to be a slightly bigger fish.

There were fish bubbling well at 12.0 and twice the lines drew suddenly taut on two of the rods. At 12.55 a swan glided straight through the swim, but a neat shot with the blow-pipe bounced a mud pellet in a curving flight, straight into his port side. He let out a small gasp of disgust and heaved himself rapidly away!

I had a stroll round the pool and was glad to discover that the dopey-looking fish up in the shallows *wasn't* my 25 mirror. It was a common of between 15 and 20 lb. There were one or two other commons, feeding close to Wasp Island. I knew I could catch one if I went and got my rod. But I wasn't bothered. Had they been really huge, I would obviously have made the effort; as it was, I was just glad to get back to my pitch and make myself a last, welcome cup of tea. It tasted a bit rich - probably something to do with the algae-thick water I was using.

Buzzards mewed, a kingfisher flew past, the sun came out and I thought, reluctantly, about packing for home. At 3.0 a family group came down from the big house and took the punt out. Definitely time to go!

Looking up from a page of writing, I watched them paddle past me. There was a hiss - which stopped dead. But the line was still tight, and as it tightened further I struck and, once more, I was amazed at the ease with which I'd set the hook.

A fast-running fish headed towards the punt like a torpedo. I brought it nicely up to the surface as it neared the starboard bow and there were shouts of exclamation from the jolly boatmen. It swung round to the right, over fifty yards out, and shot up the pool, the rod swinging round after it. I thought it must be a largish specimen: the pull was so severe and deep, and all the pressure I was applying made very little difference to it. Suddenly, after coming right in under Pitchfords and making it very difficult to keep the line clear of the alder on my right, the fish swung out again and rolled on the top. It wasn't big at all! It was a 'double' common, pulling around a mass of weed twice as big as it, but pulling it strongly - and bravely. It took a while before I got it up over the mesh. A fine, bold common - just over 10 lb.

The boaters came in for a closer look at the object of all the excitement. They were all delighted. Then I let it go so that it swam off under the punt and they watched intently as it vanished into the depths.

Though fish began to bubble and the afternoon began to look distinctly promising, after the boatmen had gone home for tea I had to pack up. It was already late, but I could hardly complain. One of my most memorable visits to Redmire - even though it was one of the shortest. And, in a way, it was nice to leave at that moment.

Thursday, 8th September - Savay Lake

Left after tea, buzzing easily through the confusing roads to the vast lake that has a river on its south side, a canal to the north, a railway to the east and poplar-lined road to the west. The lake itself is surrounded by willows and alders. It is a young lake, though. The willows are large but not yet mature and the banks, though overgrown, can't have had fishermen treading them for more than forty years - and what's forty years to a piece of landscape?

Though not yet mellow, the air seems to have a certain sense of relief; the atmosphere is like a calm oasis when you think that the crazy-paving of London begins over the next horizon. Yet some of that paving - or at least the gravel underlay - was the reason for this lake's existence.

A dark shape was blundering about on the banks, grunting and grumbling as it searched for something on the muddy ground. It was almost night, so I couldn't see what all the commotion was about. Suddenly the dark shape looked up and realised I was standing close by (it hadn't heard me as I crept up between the trees).

"Hello there, kid," it said in a Lincolnshire accent.

"How are you doing, Rod?" I said, realising I'd stumbled on the person I'd come forty miles to see.

"No good," he said. "Andy beat me to the swim I wanted to fish. I've made a new pitch here, but I'm not confident."

We were soon gabbling merrily - though we walked as we talked and ended up in the nearby pub. Over a few pints, Rod, Stuart the Bailiff, Andy the Quick and I talked about the summer's national carp events.

At 11.30 we noticed the pub had become empty and that the landlord was looking rather bored. We trundled off back to the lake and I began to set up a pitch on the opposite side of the point from which Rod was fishing. I'd just fixed up a rod when he came round and demanded a cup of tea.

We sat and talked about carp, then more mundane aspects of life, such as work, home, money, international tensions, domestic crises and death. By the time we'd finished our conversation (and three mugs of tea), it was only two hours till dawn. When it was light, I woke Rod, who was snoring in his bivouac, and stole some of his bait. Then I cast two rods from the extreme end of the point, putting the baits just short of the tree'd island about fifty yards away.

At 10.0, as two of Rod's pals, Lenny and Paul, came to report on the fishing elsewhere, and as I filled the kettle for them, I saw my silver paper flying to the butt ring of the rod. Leaping forward, I reeled in and struck and carried on reeling. The rod went firmly over and a slow-moving fish began to come in towards me, though angling slightly to the left. I kept the pressure on as Rod came running up with the net.

"Ho-ho Yatesy's into one! Is it a cod?"

The fish stayed deep and low but I thought I'd see something as it came to within about thirty feet from us. It just began to swing out into the open lake when the hook went and the bomb (a big one) flicked up through the surface.

"Bugger!"

We all went off to the local café for a greasy breakfast and a watery cup of tea. When we got back, conditions were still good - grey with a steady breeze blowing into our end of the lake. But as the day progressed, the wind dropped and the sun came out. I snoozed on the bank while I waited for the weather to change. By tea-time things seemed to be improving. The sky looked ominous and the breeze was getting up again. I left Rod (and another friend of his, Kempy, who'd just arrived) to look after my rods while I went to phone Clare and tell her I wasn't coming home after all that evening.

When I got back, my right-hand rod had had a run! Kempy said he thought I'd been using electrical irritators - the idiot - so he'd been listening out for a 'beep' and not a 'hiss', though he did mention that my kettle had been boiling for a 'long, long time'. Berk!

I re-cast, then went to share a bottle of wine with Rod (my rods were in earshot and eyeshot). The cloudy sky began to break up; slowly the wind dropped and the lake grew absolutely flat calm. The moon appeared, high above the trees on the far bank. Its reflection was perfect behind the black blades of the reeds.

The wine was the correct vintage for a warm, still, moony night. The talk was subdued; I felt any words were unnecessary. We were sitting on a ledge at the end of the world and everything in sight was thousands of miles away. I just wanted to observe the quiet beauty of the scene.

At about 10.30 (after a walk to the pub to get some food), I turned in and fell asleep as if dropping from a roof.

I was woken just before dawn by a crashing, grunting, swishing and mad reeling. Rod had struck into a fish. I jumped up and stumbled round.

"Me hands!" he said, "they won't work!"

His rheumatic joints - product of too many misty mornings - were playing him up, yet somehow he was managing, even though his twelve foot rod was curved into a circle and the line was chiming like wire. The fish made a long, curving run into a leaning willow bank, over to our left - but, with all the pressure on, Rod swung it back into open water. I got the net ready and, after one miss (the dim shape of a large carp turning at the last moment with a big splash), I lifted and safely enmeshed it. It felt quite heavy, and looked very big in the torchlight, yet I was surprised when the balance almost touched 30; in fact, 29 lb 10 oz. A leather in beautiful shape.

While drinking a fourth cup of coffee with Rod, two hours later, my line sneaked away and something ran me into the marginal trees of the distant island! That made three chances missed. Still - next time!

Monday, 21st September - The Wells

Sat in the van in the car park for ten minutes, reading the paper as the rain hammered down on the roof. Walking down to the carp pool, the trees were dripping heavily, though the sky was beginning to clear. I'd brought some new bait - floating 'cat-rings'. I sprinkled a shower over the water. But the carp didn't seem enthusiastic. They just moved about in their normal, slow, aloof, unapproachable manner. I cast to one, allowing the drift to take the hookful of rings right past its head. It bolted! It didn't go far, though and something in its appearance persuaded me to try again (not just the fact that it was above average size).

I cast again, after moving down the bank a few yards, and as the drift brought the bait down to the carp, I purposefully looked away. When I glanced back, the fish was testing a leaf. I knew it would take. It moved over to another leaf, tested it, then moved to the bait and took it straight down without hesitation. I gave it a second then struck.

"Ho-ho!" I thought, "You'll never reach the lilies from here!" But there was something else on the bottom I didn't know about, and it could have been a major tragedy when the fish dived under a deeply sunken branch. Gentle see-sawing gradually coaxed it free, and after one spectacular run across the pool it came walloping into the net. 13 ¼ lb.

Thursday, 25th September - River Kennet, Aldermaston

A cold morning, more like November than September, put the brakes on my eagerness to get out and start fishing. I was just about to leave - at about 10 a.m. - when *Angling* phoned. It was Bruce Vaughn and he wanted some chub pictures for my latest article.

"I'm just off to catch one - I'll take my camera!"

"Take a stamped, addressed envelope too," added Bruce.

Picked up Jasper on the way - then on to his chub stretch. The sun was burning away the grey layers as we drove. By the time we reached the Kennet it was blazing and hot with only a few clouds remaining - big, slow pink ones that sailed along the northern horizon.

The bit of river we'd come to fish had everything: a weir, fast shallows, slow backwaters, deep glides. As Jasper tackled up, I cast a grain of corn into the shallows below the weir and instantly hooked a small chub. Next cast, the line again skittered tight across the surface and the strike produced a slightly larger fish - about 1 lb. It fought enthusiastically!

There were no more from the shallow run and, somehow, I didn't warm to the idea of fishing the turbulent weir. So as J. cast out, I wandered down the backwater - dropping in here and there. I came to a confluence with another sidestream. Things looked more promising up this other slow-moving stretch, and in a few minutes I found the place with the right 'feel': a deep, dark bit of water under the shade of some alders. No one had fished there before. I dropped in a few grains, then cast three on my gold hook. The line settled and hung slack below the rod tip. I knew I'd only have to wait a few moments. Quietly, the loose line seemed to unwind on the surface and then draw gently tight. I tapped the rod. The Avocet bowed over and a deep, slow-moving fish circled on the bottom. It went round and round, and as it did I whistled for Jasper. As he came across the sunny field with the net, the fish rose and showed itself to be a good chub. It splashed, then took a dive for the alder roots and I had to lean out to hold it off with the long rod. It bolted across the river and I let it go. Then up it came to the surface again as Jasper arrived. Gently, I slid the fish over the net ring and, as we lifted, the hook dropped into the mesh.

After posing for *Angling Magazine*, it swam off - a bit blearily, but none the worse for its escapade. A fine conditioned, bright coloured fish. $3\frac{1}{2}$ lb.

I had my lunch by the weir pool, watching Jasper miss one or two nibbles on his ledgered pork pie, then, when I'd downed a welcome bottle of Guinness, I went back to the little slack under the alders and cast again, slightly upstream. As the line swung its angle from the tip to about $45°$, it suddenly and smoothly tightened. A spirited fight resulted in a 2 pounder. No more bites there, so I moved up, passing a little open swim and coming to a nice eddy where the water slowly swirled against a bank of alder roots. After a handful of grains went in, I cast and the bait sank slowly and became entwined in the quiet whirl of the current.

The line swung in, then out as the slow turbulence affected the bait. It swung in again, then out and kept swinging - tightening as it did so. A gentle strike and I was into my fifth chub. This one kept low, moving sullenly and occasionally pushing hard so that the rod top curved and bent viciously. I whistled as the fish made a dive for the roots, and once more the now thoroughly bored Jasper came over the field with the net.

"Why didn't we bring two?" he complained. The fish rolled; I saw it was a good one. It rushed away and I let it go - across the stream, then round and into the bank, down by a raft of nasty sticks and bits. Back it came, low and deep, then up and into the net without the expected final surge, though it thrashed about in the mesh. This was the last of the day - just 3¾ lb - though by its length, it should've been over 4. It had a very thin wrist to the tail. Took the last two frames on my roll of film, then went off to catch the last post with it. (Hope they're good enough for *Angling*.)

The day's work complete, we drove down to a different stretch, a few miles away. We had to park the van at the top of a stony lane then walk about half a mile down to the river. We could hear it as we approached: a great rush of water that we discovered was coming from not only the known whirlpool, but also another weir, a mill-race, a sluice and other assorted sidestreams. The area round a lovely old mill-house was a maze of rushing currents. The high water, after the recent rain, obviously increased the ceaseless roar.

The stretch we could fish was, unfortunately, upstream of the weir, but although the river was less intimate than the sidestream I'd been fishing previously, there were one or two chubby-looking swims. But the chub were not so easy to fool - at least the ones that found my bait. They tweaked it, pulled at it, gave all sorts of gentle hints at the rod end, but I couldn't hit one.

I shouldn't have free-lined, what with the swift current. I did change to a light ledger - but even then I couldn't hit the little runts. I should've float fished in the deep slacks. There may even have been a chance for my first barbel.

The sun glowed on the poplars on the far bank and the scene around was one of pastoral beauty and richness. As the sun set, a thin ground mist began to creep across the fields behind me.

I finally caught a ½ lb chub from under a bush and I was almost as pleased about him as I was with the near 4 pounder! Jasper was poaching in the weir and I went down to see him land a 1 lb chub and a terrific gudgeon. The mist in the fields began to thicken so that only the heads of the cows were showing.

We walked back, over the wooden bridges and away from the sound of water, along the quiet leafy lane. It was almost dark by the time I swung the van out on to the homeward road.

Monday, 29th September

Finished writing a chapter for Rod's book and, after I'd posted it (and had some tea), I went down to the Wells. Just before sunset it was, on a grey, very still, very warm evening. The water was strewn with fallen leaves and I looked between them, searching for those dark shapes below the surface. But I only found one. I cast for it, after chucking out a few samples of 'fish rings'. As I did so, a vague figure appeared under the vague trees. It was Clare! She'd walked down from the cottage, liking the feel of the evening and tired of doing her *Angling* cover. I'd driven down, though, and she'd got there - on foot - before I made my first cast! Maybe she is an angel after all - or a witch!

We sat under the tall ash tree and the evening deepened, making the pool seem wider and longer. The bats fluttered round our heads.

After half an hour the silver paper scraped across the path where we sat and I snatched up the Avocet and struck, sweeping the rod over to the left. There was a brief curve on the tip as I felt a good weight - then all went slack.

That's the first time I've missed on the strike at the Wells. Let's hope it's the last.

Tuesday, 30th September

Encouraged by Clare's quick arrival on foot yesterday, I set off at 11 a.m. - also on foot - with just the usual rod and net and a pocketful of bits. The woods were just beginning to glow - the leaves smouldering on the edge of autumn. The sun was warm.

Arrived at the pool so quickly, and the walk was so much more pleasant than the two-mile drive, that I couldn't think how I'd used the van all those times before.

The carp were enjoying the late September heat and a bunch of them were lying among the remains of the lily-bed as I sneaked up under the trees and cast a piece of Purina at them. They weren't all that interested. I tried macaroni - they weren't impressed at all. I moved to the next set of pads and there, after a heart-stopping wait, in which I had to turn away (laughing - so great was the tension), a floating smelly drifted right onto the nose of a double-figure carp, who suddenly sucked it down. I flexed instinctively and brought the rod up a few inches, ready to strike as soon as the head went down. But the carp just spat the bait out, almost instantly. I cursed and trembled. There were three fish underneath those pads and they all just looked at the bait - with a bored, though slightly suspicious expression.

Up in the shallows I had a chance offered me on a plate. A fish rose and began slipping through the mat of fallen leaves, right under my nose. But I'd cast out next to the reeds, where I'd seen another fish move, and of course by the time I'd gently reeled in, the carp beneath my feet had disappeared.

All day I cast and stalked. The sun was hot and the fish stayed on the top. A couple of northern boneheads were fishing from the dam and though there were carp moving down there, I couldn't face fishing for them. The northernites had a bloody radio play-ing bonehead music and it was too polluted with poisonous sounds at the deep end.

The sun moved off the water, the fish began to look more interested. I said to myself I was going to catch one - but I shouldn't tempt luck and fate into scorning me. I wasn't going to catch one.

Two old ladies walked quietly past me. One said to the other: "It was in September."

In September, I only caught a single carp.

Thursday, 2nd October - Redmire

Sat quietly by the fire, after packing the van with tackle and gear, a glass of whisky in my hands, Satie's piano music lulling my ears. It was a cold, clear evening and I felt no need to rush off to the pool. Clare almost persuaded me to stay on for supper.

It was even colder at Bernithan. A thick mist had been lying across the fields by the Wye and, though I'd risen up out of it as I came through Glewstone, dropping down to the pool I found the mist again.

John made me some tea and described his previous, dramatic night. Three fish landed - to 23 lb; one huge fish lost round an un-known snag. All week he's been fishing, yet all the action came on that one night - not a touch until then. Bait was small pieces of luncheon meat!

I set up in the Evening Pitch (again) and it must've been the coldest night I've been out in. Even in my big army bag I could feel the chill penetrating, keeping me from sleep. So I threw my old green bag over the top of me and that was enough to start the temperature rising comfortably.

Friday, 3rd October

Should've got up properly at dawn, instead of just blearily casting out the Avon and then diving back into the warmth of the sleeping-bag. It was a beautiful, slow-rolling mist cloud of a dawn and it would've made a fair picture as the sun rose. As it was, I slept till 10 a.m!

Up under Greenbanks I found a group of 'big double' commons and cast for them without success. There seemed to be quite a few fish feeding up in the shallows and I spent all afternoon up there - casting from the climbing stump with a light quill float and corn. One or two very big carp moved close by, just dark shapes in the sunlit, breeze-rippled water. There was a good deal of truffling going on and my float shot away two or three times - but I missed every bite. I think small fish were to blame; I could see a small shoal of what looked like $1/2$ lb carp, the smallest fish I've seen here for years. I think it was them doing most of the truffling, though they certainly attracted the bigger fish into the area by their activity. I wonder, having said that, whether a rake-up is a feasibility. It's anarchic enough to make me want to try!

Moved round to the Black Quill Pitch as the sun began to sink, and fished there until almost dark. Had one chance as a group of carp went by, but the biggest fish were bubbling just out of range and I couldn't get them to come in.

That night, after an evening sky the colour of smouldering coal, a dense cloud cover kept the temperature up and I thought a fish was going to oblige. But hardly a sound broke the silence of the pool. Not a fish rolled or leapt - not like the previous, freezing cold night.

Saturday, 4th October

Everything is on a grand scale at Redmire, even sleep, which is why I woke late and groggily. The wind was blowing into the dam. Ideal for a bit of float fishing, sitting on the rail. The breeze was cool and I moved out of the shadows in the corner and fished in the sunlight, behind the Bush. The quill never even bobbed.

Up in the shallows, I found a group of commons hanging about by the leaning willow. I tossed two free grains of corn at them and they bolted!

Dave Bufton came down to tell me that there were some huge fish moving slowly along in front of the Evening Pitch and Pitchfords. They were bubbling too, so I went back to my pitch and fished for them for a while. Then, at 4.20, I drove into Ross for some new bait. Had a hunch cockles would do it - though I was going to make up some ground rice and rennet essence. Couldn't be bothered in the end and, anyway, I fancied a quick change of scene.

Went into an old book shop while I was in the town and bought two thirds of their angling collection. They only had three volumes on the shelves and the two I bought were lovely - I've not heard of either before and I got change from £2. Not bad. Both are written in the same gentle Edwardian style of my favourite books. Almost as good as a carp. (*A Rod in Hand* by C.V. Hancock and *Fishes I Have Known* by A. Beavan.)

Back at the pool, I had some tea while the cockles defrosted in the last of the sun. Then I cast as the sun went down, feeling sure, yet not staying by my rods, like I should've done. It's happened too often before - I go round and talk with someone next door and a fish comes round to my rods but leaves before I can rush back and strike. Ah, for a bit of solitude - then I wouldn't get invitations for tea.

The worst of it is, I know I shouldn't leave my pitch, even for a moment, and often get an empty feeling within if I do so.

As I talked with Barry (who'd arrived last night) and John in the Ruins, the penny dropped from my spool across the pool and landed 'plonk' on a dish I'd placed below. We heard it clearly and I cursed and ran round to find only a few yards of line gone. It could've been an eel. But it could've been what I'd been waiting for.

Made some supper and nearly blew up my bivouac with a leaking stove! Read *Drop me a Line* until the candle faded and died.

Sunday, 5th October

Woke to a misty dawn. Re-baited and re-cast the rods. As the morning progressed, one or two patches of bubbles began to rise. It was growing noticeably warmer, too. Everything looked very promising as we three packed up at noon and had to leave for home.

Tuesday, 21st October - Redmire

It's been so cold and the weather so bloody awful, haven't had even an afternoon's fishing since that last trip here. But with the month suddenly mild and almost muggy, prospects began to look favourable for this very short, and possibly last, session of the year.

Arrived a day later than planned, which was extremely slack of me, as Monday was a glorious day - bright, and warm and very still. Today was still warm, but it wasn't early when I got here - 3 p.m. - so I didn't have long to make the most of it.

I tackled up immediately - Avon 3, float tackle and maggots. Then I went up to the shallows. It was a breezy, restless day and the pool looked unfamiliar after the cold storms of the previous week. There were only a few leaves left on the black poplars and the oaks were a dull ochre. The willows were shedding their foliage - yellow leaves lay in the grass like great shoals of beached goldfish.

There were no carp visible on the east bank - or from the platform on the other side. But from the Island Tree I could see, vaguely, one or two large fish moving just off the fallen willow. One of them was the colour of an autumn beech-leaf.

I'd thrown out some maggots just off the island and, looking down, I thought I could see small clouds of red mud. Were fish feeding on the groundbait? Quickly I descended the tree and cast a float out over the apparent disturbance. For an hour I waited, but the orange quill never moved. I climbed the tree again and the vague clouds were still there. Perhaps it was gudgeon, or eels. A big common cruised past quite close. Then another. I watched them heading up into the shallows and I followed them, after climbing down the Island Tree, then shimmying up the Platform Tree. But all I could see from there were floating leaves.

It was beginning to look like evening. Behind a purple layer of high cloud, the sun was getting low. I thought about it for a while, then decided to set up in Inghams. Perhaps only because it was my favourite late season pitch - perhaps also because I had no strong inclination to fish anywhere else. I'd thought about Pitchfords - but then decided no. By the time I'd put up the bivouac and tackled up with my other two rods, it was dark. Making the bait had taken longer than I'd anticipated. It was the first paste bait I've used here. Ground rice, fish meal, eggs and essence of rennet! Gor! With ingredients like that, how can I fail? I boiled some of it up to give the baits a bit of a skin - but I think the unboiled version is better. (Not only is essential food value destroyed by cooking, there is also a term for a boiled bait that I heard recently:

'boilies'! Like calling floating crusts 'bakies'!) Discovered I'd forgotten my teapot! Aghast, I had to make my tea in the pressure-cooker. I bet that's a record.

By candlelight, I read *The Guardian*, then finished my Mk II Christmas article for *Angling*. Ended up giggling with the ludicrous plot. As I wrote, it began to pour down. The raindrops drummed heavily on the canvas.

Wednesday, 22nd October

After a warm night, dreaming of a big common at Burgh Heath Pond, I woke to rain and a stormy-looking morning. Slept through half of it - my usual 'first morn at Redmire drowsiness' had overcome me. I re-cast, made tea (with less difficulty than last night), then finished the 'fair-copy' of the Christmas story. Timed it just nicely and was in Langarren for the 3.30 post. Phoned Clare - then back to the windy pool as the rains stopped. Cast out again. Had tea. Not a fish moved anywhere. A brilliant moon broke through the cloud at around 8.30. Coming out from candlelight, the moonlight seemed brighter. The ducks seemed to have a lot to laugh about - they were probably laughing at me, fishing at the wrong end of the pool.

At midnight, a great flock of rooks went over, cawing loudly. I looked up into the sky, but couldn't see them. Turned to sleep then, hearing just the faint streak of sound of the odd redwing, flying under the stars.

Woke during the night to a furious wind. My canvas was billowing and wobbling, but everything held firm.

Thursday, 23rd October

Cast out at 8.30 a.m. - and there was I, thinking I was going to make a 7.0 start! The wind still blew. A carp rolled opposite the Fence.

I waited till about 10.30, reading the classic 'Cunning Carp' chapter, then went up to have a look off the island. The wind was lessening and the sky breaking. Beneath the ripples I thought I could see a dark, motionless carp-shape. It was huge and I was reminded immediately of the big leather I saw in the same position, at the same time of year, back in '77. Then the sun shone and the fish moved nearer. It *was* the leather - the Black Queen! It was heading very slowly up the pool and by the time I'd crept off to snatch up the Avon 3, bait with maggots, grab the net and return to the island, the fish had only gone a few yards. I could see it easily moving just off the Island Tree, low on the bottom.

I made a stupid mistake and tried to cast from the left of the island, lessening the distance. But the leaning branches made the cast extremely difficult and accuracy was all important. I should've seen the error and gone back to the right of the island. But I cast anyway and the bait landed four feet to the rear of the carp's tail. Would he turn? Of course not! He - no, she - just kept inching along the bottom. I reeled in and I saw that now the cast was truly impossible. The carp had gone past the tips of the branches. So I had to change position. Why hadn't I done it in the first place?

It was a much easier cast and the bait flew nice and easy - but dropped just long; the line was lying over the carp's back! Naturally, she didn't like that, although she didn't bolt, just cruised off for a yard or two - well out of reach.

I went up the tree, taking the rod with me, and I cast for the third time at the monster. I was right at the top of the tree and though I couldn't see clearly, I'm pretty sure the fish came right over the bait. A wind blew and the ripples obscured my sight. The next thing I knew, the big carp was heading slowly away, going past Keffords, following the same course as 30th October '77. Quickly, I hurried round to my pitch and cast the rods so that the bait would be lying in the path of the monster. But these things only happen once in a lifetime. I'd had my chance three years ago and muffed it. I wasn't going to get another go. Still, it was reassuring to see 'B.Q.' again, to be reminded of just how vast a creature she was. I had a better view of her this time, which only confirmed my first impressions: there is no denying how much bigger she is than the Bishop.

At 1.0, I went for a stroll down to the little pond to see the carp there. The bigger of the two was right in the margins - he looked as if he'd just come out from a hole in the mud. As I got back to my pitch, Dave Short arrived. We had a chat, over a cup of tea, then, as I'd not got more than three hours left, I stole some bronze maggots off him and went for a look in the shallows. I saw a big commotion - but it wasn't a fish feeding, it was a fish dying. Another strange coincidence, too. This unfortunate fish was the 24 lb mirror I'd caught almost exactly eight years ago to the day. Dave netted it out - but we didn't kill it. It seemed as if it might recover, though its head was swollen horribly. We left it in deep water, off the Boathouse. Then I went back to the shallows.

From the end of the fallen branch, I watched my orange quill bobbing in the incoming ripples. Some bubbles appeared, but they didn't look carpy. I cast again, tossing some maggots round the float. More bubbles rose and this time I was sure they *were* carp. The quill half sank and I grabbed the rod - but didn't strike. Eventually the float rose again and I put the rod back on the willow bough.

The sun was almost hot, though the breeze kept things cool. The poor old mirror suddenly appeared again in the margins -

right underneath me. I looked back at the float and it was gone. I struck and felt a delicious resistance. The rod wound over and the fish made two or three long lunges away from me. The water swirled, but didn't break, though I heaved and tried to get the above-pressure to bring the carp up to the top. Stupidly, I let him run and he went flying past the willow down the bank, then turned sharp left and lunged into the margin, right among the drooping branches. Dave came running along, with net and waders. He said he could see it - but it wasn't very big. So I heaved for all I was worth, which obviously isn't much today. The hook came free!

Gumboils! Just a small one would've been fine, what with it being time to go. I cast again and left the float for an hour. The bough became extremely uncomfortable and the quill never moved.

27th November - River Rother, Fittleworth

The weather and my inclination were not conducive to fishing over the past three or four weeks - but today, it had been previously arranged with *two* others that I should go chub fishing with them. So I couldn't get out of it, whatever the weather or my inclination.

As it turned out, the weather broke, bright and mild after a freezing night and my mood, after a couple of (successful) visits to London, inclined naturally riverwards.

The sun was just being obscured by a cloud as Julian and I arrived on the bank where Roy was already fishing. He'd already had two chubs! Both about 2 lb. He was fishing the Three Fishes, where I'd hoped to start Julian off. But Julian fished the Dead Swan instead - though this was difficult as, since last season, another big branch (more like a tree trunk) has swung into the eddy and now lies directly across its middle, like a half-submerged crocodile. Julian didn't get a touch.

I tried up- and downstream and got not a touch. Also the pubs closed before we'd even remembered them, so we didn't have any lunch. Clouds began to gather in the west and the wind began to get thin and sharp. My hands began to get paralysed.

At 3.0 I felt a bit better, Julian having gone off to get provisions from the village stores. But it was a while before I began to thaw out. I decided to accelerate the warming process and throw my hat around the field. Julian joined in the sport, and we were just getting into the swing of it when we heard a shout from up the bank; it was Roy, coming down the bank with a full landing net. 4 lb 2 oz. A beauty.

The sun began to burn the horizon red and the sky completely cleared of cloud. It was a cold, transparent blue. I moved from the Three Fishes (Roy had long departed from that swim) up to the Dead Swan (Jules had long departed from that one). Getting into position and putting on an $1/8$ oz bomb. I cast over the 'crocodile' and let the current swing the tackle clear, so that the bait (luncheon meat) was a few feet from the downstream alder roots, in the quiet water and out of the main flow. Second or third cast, the rod tip jerked over and I struck - but missed. Re-baiting, I cast again, holding a loop of line and feeling for bites with my gloved hand. I didn't need to hold the line. The rod was smoothly and forcefully bent over, and this time I couldn't miss. But, like a fool, I struck holding on to the loop and, as I was wearing gloves, I didn't want to try and shake the line free of my fingers - so I just hung on and hoped. Everything felt remote and awkward.

At first I didn't give the fish much stick. I hoped it would run downstream, away from the treacherous 'crocodile'. It didn't; it ran towards me, under the great bar of wood. With the rod tip held almost in the water, I kept my adversary on an easy line, let him pull and bore about *under* the snags. The sensations of jarring and rubbing were awful. Eventually, I bent into it a bit more and felt something coming through the barrier of sunken timber.

I could hardly believe it when it suddenly all came clear. I was almost sure I was going to lose him. A dark back broke surface, then I saw a silver flank. A big chub! He dived suddenly under the flotsam that lined the bank and once more the line struck a snag - a big log this time. Again I worked it free. He dived straight down and all went solid for a moment, but it was only the force of momentum, holding it steady at the end of the thrust. Back he came to the surface again, then again into the flotsam, then made a bolt towards the 'crocodile'. All the time I had to draw and loosen the loop of line while I would've been much happier playing the fish on the reel. Ah well, the rod was responding well, bowed over, relaxing slightly, then bent hard as the chub dived again towards midstream.

Julian arrived with the net and I told him to advance cautiously as I didn't want to risk any further sudden lunges into the snags. On 4 lb line I could only do so much. A big mouth gaped on the surface and I held it steady as Julian reached out gently and slowly. I eased it in an extra foot and then it was ours. A long, silver slab of chub lay in the cold blue afterglow.

If it hadn't tapered so suddenly from the pelvic to the tail it would probably have gone over 5, but I was well pleased with the $4^1/_2$ lb it did pull. I showed it to Roy, then released it by a bed of dead rushes. It swam off well enough.

The light seemed to visibly darken as I fished a last half hour. One or two good 'thunks' hit the rod top, but I didn't hit anything in return. A sea trout leapt clear of the water and fell back with a 'sperlosh!' Its flanks flashed steel grey. Roy wandered down to say it was nearly opening time. It was just light enough for a couple more casts and I did get one terrific bite. But again, nothing on the strike.

We all three packed up then and walked slowly off back to the bridge, under the stars. At the Welldiggers a large lazy fire was blazing. And the ale was good.

Saturday, 7th February - River Rother, Fittleworth

This is the fourth time since that last November day that I've fished the river. Each time, although there've been chances, I've blanked. High water, low water, it made no difference - the only thing that was consistent was a strong breeze, cooling if not cold, and I was always fishing in the afternoons until dark. Obviously, these are points to remember and avoid. So, today, I'd set my heart on an early start, hoping to be on the water-meadows before the wind.

The alarm failed and I didn't set off till 11.45! It was a mild, grey spring-like morning in the Vale and, when I stopped for petrol at Petworth, a blackbird was singing like April. I went to the tackle shop to buy a new spool of line for the Aerial and I got talking to a blonde about the glories of the Barbour jacket, so I was further delayed.

At the bridge at Fittleworth I discovered Ron Lally tackling up for a pike. It was four years since we'd last met and by the time we'd finished our exchange of greetings another hour had flown by. Tom arrived, complaining about the bitter downstream wind. I thought it was time to start fishing.

With my newly made swan-quill, I'd planned to swim the stream at the Three Fishes - but that downstream wind was as bad as Tom had described. The new float was blown flat. I gave up after a while and ledgered, hooking something after ten minutes that snagged me across the river. I had to pull for a break.

Bloody hell! It was beginning to get dark and I hadn't even got into my rhythm. Dave arrived from downstream. He'd had three small ones and lost a few larger ones. He wandered off back to the bridge. I fished into the sinking light and the wind never eased at all, though I was beginning to get hardened to it and began to grow resistant to the cold. I thought I'd get a fish in the dark, up at the Dead Swan. On the third cast, the bait and lead went over an alder branch and that was that.

Drove home suffering from a strange vacancy of mind.

26th February - River Rother, Fittleworth

One year, less a day, since that memorable outing with Rick and Roy. Roy had booked today for the river and I'd said I could make it too. But the morning was the coldest and bleakest of the winter - frost under a grey sky - so I didn't hurry. Anyway, I was finishing a picture of a carp leaping at Milton Mount. Should've arrived earlier than 3.20, though. Roy said they'd been biting all day! He'd only had one, though; a 2 pounder. He'd hoped that I was going to arrive in time for a pub lunch - as I did last week (another blank!). It wasn't so much that he was thirsty - he was freezing.

By the time I'd tackled up at Dead Swan (there was another one there today - it must be something in the way the river bends that distresses those birds), my fingers were burning with cold. Though there was only a slight and intermittent breeze, it wrapped round me like a frosted shroud. No bites on crust or prawn. Moved to the Three Fishes. No bites on float or prawn. Moved up to Roy's Run. No bites. The Bight. No bites. Roy packed up and stalked past me in the deepening grey evening. At least we found a blazing log fire to sit next to - trouble was, a family at a table next to us was eating grilled steak and chips and we only had enough pennies for a pint each and a shared packet of crisps.

Monday, 9th March - Wadesmarsh Pond

Rick had just come back from a week's salmon fishing in Scotland and was eager to catch fish on this, the last day of his holiday. He'd blanked, of course. It was mild, very mild. We'd go chubbing. But it was pouring as we drove down to Fittleworth and it had poured all night. We had to detour because of the rain. First to the Black Horse, Byworth, for a spot of lunch etc. Then down to the Rother. One look was enough. It was heaving down, only just within its banks. So we drove back along the maze of lanes that lead to Wadesmarsh.

We set up, after a quick stroll round the slippery banks, by the remains of a last summer's reed-bed, and we had to fish together as it was still raining hard and we only had one brolly. I'd bought some corn in Petworth *and* a little bottle of almond essence which I, accidentally, half emptied into the tin so I had to wash it around a bit and drain the can a couple of times. Then we began fishing, casting our quill floats just beyond the dead reeds and a little to the right of them. I sat back, watching the grey sky hurrying over, watching the rain dimpling the wind-blown pool. Then after quarter of an hour my red-tipped swan-quill just sank. I picked up the Avocet and gently set the hook. It was a carp! It went slowly into the rotting reeds and stuck, but gentle, steady pressure began to move it, and finally I had that lovely free movement on the line as the fish came clear. Not for long though. I was just about to commence the proper open-water-battle, when the line broke! It had caught somehow against the foot of the old Aerial, and as I tugged it to free it, it snapped. I saw it catch in the wind and fly through the rings. Desperately I tried to grab it as it caught for a moment in a hawthorn on my right. But I grabbed Rick's line instead of mine. My newly painted swan-quill disappeared into the depths.

Ten minutes later, with another (black-tipped) swan-quill, I watched as it slid under, then I struck - and missed. But soon it moved again, sliding beautifully away to the left and bobbing under as it went. Couldn't miss, and once more it dived into the reeds. It must have taken five minutes to ease it up to the last nasty clump where I couldn't free it. Rick leaned forward, with the net at full extension, and the carp bolted. Luckily the line didn't snap - the reed stems did. With the float, the tangle of reed went shooting out into the pool. Not bad, I thought, for 3 lb b.s. Platil! After a bit, I swung him into the net, only Rick lifted far too soon and brought the head of the carp up on the rim. It somersaulted off, amid roars of laughter from Rick, who then tried to scoop it back into the mesh. The carp didn't like this and ran like a crazed hare out and then down to the reeds along the bank to our right. After a wild argument he came back, the rod bent nicely. This time we got him; a leather the colour of a goldfish - 5 lb.

Rick just had to catch one and I suggested putting a bait out over the reeds to our left. He did and, while having a pee, his float went down. After a game struggle, out came another leather of equally glorious coloration. $4\frac{1}{2}$ lb. Then he hooked and lost a better one; then he landed a small gold wildie. The rain still poured, the wind still blew. Rick began to lose sight of his float in the evening gloom, but I could see my black one easily (I'd moved down to the next reed-bed). But we were cold and wet and it was time for tea, so we packed up, happy with our day and our chub-sized carp.

Wednesday, 11th March - Wadesmarsh

It stopped raining as I drove through Haslemere, and the sky was brightening when I got to the pond a few minutes later. I'd tackled up the Avocet at home and so all I had to do (after replacing missing shot) was to swing the tackle out by the dead reeds again and sit down on the muddy bank to watch my black-tipped quill. The wind was less strong, the ripples were less troublesome than before. After about twelve minutes, the float bobbed and moved and I picked up the rod in anticipation. Nothing happened for a moment, then the quill slid steadily away to the left and down. I struck, and the rod curved over. After a few seconds, there was a big splash and a hefty boil and I knew this one was a bit bigger than the carp of Monday. I tried to ease him away from the reeds, but he was in them in no time, churning through the old stems, and eventually getting the line neatly threaded through the fibres of the reed furthest from me. I could bring the fish to the surface, mouth gulping, but he wouldn't come clear and I felt there was no hope for the 3 lb line as he bolted away, causing a nasty grating sensation to run down the rod. Incredibly, the line held for the numerous dives and plunges and it seemed that if I could get the net to him, I might succeed after all. Somehow I managed to extend the net handle, get one boot off and step out one long pace towards the carp without losing hold of the rod. The fish dived and the reed stem bent after him like a second rod - but the line, luckily, ran through it and didn't catch and snap. I drew the carp back and, as he was lying near the surface, I got the net ring under him and lifted. I even got the line back unbroken! 7 lb, he weighed. I had to laugh.

I cast again and had three more good bites, striking one and completely missing it. The sun came out, glowing on the oaks on the far side. Their branches were a brilliant moss-green. A rabbit hopped by. I moved the tackle to the far/middle of the reed-bed and I had a lovely sinking bite within five minutes. It felt big, but as I wound down and brought some pressure to bear, there was a grating on the line and it snapped: a bite-off by the look of the line end.

The sun had set, the clouds were gathering again. Time for tea (my feet were bloody cold!)

Thursday, 12th March

The morning had been warm and bright; the birds sang, white clouds glided over. Had to finish two covers before I could leave and must have got to Wadesmarsh at 3.30 p.m. The sun was bright on the far bank (the oaks were grey, not green now), but I picked the same spot as before - the reed-bed on the cool western bank, where the eddying current of the breeze blew in my face. Set up two rods! The Avon went out with a free-line, again over the reed-bed, the Avocet's quill was dropped just off the edge. Ten minutes later the float slid under. I missed. I re-cast, close to the reeds and after about quarter of an hour it slowly submerged, angling as it did so, towards the reeds. I connected and, remembering all the previous fights, got a maximum sidestrain on. Before the carp knew what was happening, I'd got it out into open water where I had an easy time of it. The fish hardly got an inch of line. Another gold-coloured leather, 4½ lb.

Hooked a common next cast - ½ lb! Then I got a 1 lb tench. Then just after sunset, I put the quill into a new position and it gently sank after three minutes. A beautiful 2 lb wildie - the gold scales were edged with a deep olive-green. The Avon's line hadn't even twitched, even though there was a fully scaled mirror on the hook when I reeled in. It was nearly as big as the palm of my hand! The colour was as pink as the sunset clouds.

Friday, 13th March

Arrived at about 3 p.m. on another breezy, mild afternoon. Again there were flashes of sunshine, but more cloud than yesterday. I wasn't surprised to see two cars parked by the gate, or to discover three anglers - all fishing on the dam (the worst place, I should've thought). I had the Avocet still rigged up with the swan-quill, and within three minutes of arriving I'd cast out to the edge of the reed-bed and was sitting on my camp-stool, expectantly watching the float. I'd remembered to bring my gloves today which was as well, for the breeze was fresh and cool.

After about ten minutes I had the standard bite - a slow

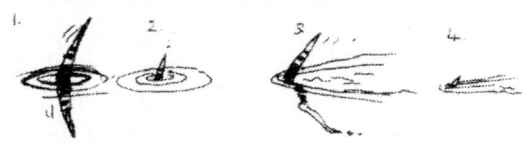

I struck to the right, getting up as I did so and holding the fish away from the far corner of the reeds. For a minute or two it plunged dangerously close, but never quite made it. I saw the turbulence smoothing the ripples as it went off into the open water. I worked him in and got the net ready. A sudden rush caught me unawares and I had to laugh, but I soon got my carp back and in a moment he was safe in the mesh. Another richly coloured leather - 5 lb.

The sky darkened and it began to rain. Two of the other fishermen, who didn't seem to have caught anything and who seemed to be suspicious at my luck, packed up. I went for a walk to warm up and went to have a look at the upper lake - a water that used to be a carp lake but has now become sullied with trout. When I got back I had to help push the two anglers' car out of a ditch. I was right - they hadn't even had a bite. (No almond essence on their corn!) Ten minutes later, the swan-quill, now positioned over the edge of the reeds, bobbed and rose and I prepared to strike. It lay still for a few seconds, then slid away and I connected with another carp. "Go out!" I willed. But he just rolled about on the very edge of the reeds. Then he moved off and I gave him some slack, moving right and lifting the line clear of one awkward stem. He was in the open now and I could relax and enjoy the fight, which was quite entertaining. One run bent the Avocet hard over and set the old reel singing, then he moved from the left, way over to the right and nearly hit a lone reed clump. 6 lb of leather carp then thrashed in the net. The third angler packed up.

The sky darkened even more and rain began to fall in fat drops that bubbled on the surface. The float sank once more and in came a ¹/₂ lb tench!

It was cold, but I didn't feel it; it was wet, but I didn't care. I ended up singing (quite loudly). On the way home I remembered I'd once caught a carp nearly ten times as big as the Wadesmarsh fish. But it didn't make them seem any less delightful. It just made me sing more loudly.

Saturday, 14th March - Shillinglee

Though I dreamt of Redmire, I couldn't make it. But I remembered Shillinglee and the willow by the boat-house. It was a beautiful day; I'd go there. It wasn't until about 5.0 that I'd cast - the sun was already low over Lythe Hill. A breeze rippled into the bay, so after a while I moved round into the sheltered water on the other side of the willow. There, just beyond a reed-bed, a patch of bubbles showed and I waited expectantly for the float to move. But it didn't. The sun set, the breeze dropped and for the first time this week I had a flat calm lake to fish. As the light began to dim I went back to my original position and put the quill out by the edge of the willow. I put the rod in its rest, then glanced across the water. Where was the float? Shall I strike? I hesitated and . . .

Curses! I re-cast but the float didn't move again, though it appeared to - materialising and dematerialising in the fading light.

A woodcock came out of the woods and flew across the fields behind me. A planet began to twinkle in reflection and the ³/₄ moon was white and beginning to throw shadows. I took off the faithful quill and cast the tackle again, putting a fold of silver foil on the line. Within seconds it jumped and I struck. I missed. I cast again and waited ten minutes before discovering the line was trapped on the rest. It was tight when I freed it and I felt a tugging as I lifted the rod. There was a small splash. Probably only a roach - but no matter - anything'll do on the last day. It got off !

I got into a bird's nest and had to fumble about with lighted matches, re-tying the hook after I'd been forced to break the line. I cast again and soon the foil began to jerk across the bank. I waited. It stopped.

So ended the last take of the season. But so what! It was a beautiful evening. The moon was bright on the lake, the owls were calling, eight swans looked like gaps in the bankside trees. A fish splashed across the bay and the coots and moorhens clucked in alarm.

"Last cast," I told myself, and flicked the bait into the still water by the bare willow. Next time, that willow will be in full leaf and the reeds will be thick and green. The carp will cruise into the shade beneath the branches and I will be waiting. Ah! What happy prospects to look forward to. And what a season to look back on. Grand beginning, memorable ending.

Not quite the ending yet, though. Just one more cast . . .

Compleat Redmire Catchlist 🐟

Type or Species	Weather	Time	Tackle & Bait	Weight or Distinguishing Features
common	Bright, warm	9.0 am	Legered Kidney Bean Mk III	27 (Shallows) (Pitchfords)
mirror	Breezy	10.30 am	10 b.s. line	25 (Evening Pitch)
mirror	Moonlight	3.30 am	Ditto, but Macaroni	
eel	Sunset		Sweet Corn. C.S. III	25 (Greenbanks)
Brown China	midsummer	9.20	Cockle	Pythonesque (35)
Common	Breezy	Teatime	Net	Spotless
mirror	Hot, breezy	3.0 pm	B. Bean. Mk IV 10 br.	27 (Wasp Island)
common	cool o/cast	9.30 am	corn legered	24 (Willow Pitch)
Common	Muggy	11.0 am	corn float	10½
Common	Rain	4.0 pm.	corn	10½ (Shallows)
Common	Sunset	8.0 pm.	"	10½ (Mostly)
Common	Thunder	2.0 am.	" "	10½
Common	Gale	5.0 p.m.	" "	10½
Common	Still, Cool.	6.0 am.	" "	18½ (Wasp Island)
common	Hot Bright	3.0 pm	maggots	
Terrapin		5.0 pm.	All-Day	Caught sight of
common	O/cast Dawn clear	?	Kidney B. Ledgered Mk III	under Bowskill's Tree 21 (Greenbanks)
Common	Sunset clear	8.0 pm.	corn f/line	16 ('35)
common	Sunrise clear	4.50 am	Truffle 1b. Mk. III b.s.	24 (Greenbanks)
Common	Sunset	9.1m	B. Bean lab. F/lined	17 (Shallows)
Mirror	Dull, damp	9.30	Corn. Avon	51
common	Drizzle	Noon	Blackberry	12 (Dam)
Gudgeon	Hot still	2.13.154	Worm Float	2½ oz. (from Punt)
mirror	settled	Dawn	B. Bean o/line	29 (Greenbanks)
Common	Dull, breezy.	P.m.	B. Bean f/line	12 (3) (Greenbanks) 13
"	Hot Bright	Teatime	Hand	49" (Shallows)
Grasssnake	Breezy	B/Fast	Cockle	(16) (Inghams)
Common	"			Anacondaesque (Dam)
Grass-snake	"	Break-fast time	Hand	24" (Evening)
Grass-snake				
Common	Dull, Breezy showers	"	Legered corn	43 (Fence)
Common	Sunset	supper time	"	16 (Willow) 14
"	Sunrise	o/cast	float	15(2) (Platform - Shallows)
"	Grey, still warm	Teatime	Being B Prawn Dawn	15 "
"	Breezy	Elevenses Teatime	Corn (Float)	14 (Dam) 17 "
Gudgeons	Still, Grey. Muggy.	"	maggots	42 (Dam)
Common	Cool, clear	Pubtime	Float & Corn	24 (Dam)
Leather	Moonlight	Boattime	K. Bean	27 (Fence) (No. 13)
Common	Bright, Hot	Elevenses	D. Biscuit	23 (Island)
Common	Clear, still	B/Fast	maggots	24 (Ashgrove)
eel	"	noon		Stupendous (5ft - 6ft) (Caught sight of from Punt)

Chris Yates